THE LYRICAL POEMS OF
FRANÇOIS VILLON

THE LYRICAL POEMS OF

FRANÇOIS VILLON

In the original French, & in the English versions by

Algernon Charles Swinburne, Dante Gabriel

Rossetti, William Ernest Henley, John

Payne, and Léonie Adams; selected

by Léonie Adams. With an

introductory essay by

Robert Louis

Stevenson

THE LIMITED EDITIONS CLUB

NEW YORK · MCMLXXIX

THE CONTENTS

FRANÇOIS VILLON

STUDENT, POET, AND HOUSEBREAKER

BY ROBERT LOUIS STEVENSON

P ERHAPS one of the most curious revolutions in literary history is the sudden bull's-eye light cast by A. Longnon on the obscure existence of François Villon. His book is not remarkable merely as a chapter of biography exhumed after four centuries. To readers of the poet it will recall, with a flavor of satire, that characteristic passage in which he bequeaths his spectacles—with a humorous reservation of the case—to the hospital for blind paupers known as the Fifteen-Score. Thus equipped, let the blind paupers go and separate the good from the bad in the cemetery of the Innocents! For his own part the poet can see no distinction. Much have the dead people made of their advantages. What does it matter now that they have lain in state beds and nourished portly bodies upon cakes and cream! Here they all lie, to be trodden in the mud; the large estate and the small, sounding virtue and adroit or powerful vice, in very much the same condition; and a bishop not to be distinguished from a lamplighter with even the strongest spectacles.

Such was Villon's cynical philosophy. Four hundred years after his death, when surely all danger might be considered at an end, a pair of critical spectacles have been applied to his own remains; and though he left behind him a sufficiently ragged reputation from the first, it is only after these four hundred years that his delinquencies have been finally tracked home, and we can assign him to his proper place among the good or wicked. It is a staggering thought, and one that affords a fine figure of the imperishability of men's acts, that the stealth of the private inquiry office can be carried so far back into the dead and dusty past. We are not so soon quit of our concerns as Villon fancied. In the extreme of dissolution, when not so much as a man's name is remembered, when his dust is scattered to the four winds, and perhaps the very grave and the very graveyard where he was laid to rest have been forgotten, desecrated, and buried under populous towns—even in this extreme let an antiquary fall across a sheet of manuscript, and the name will be recalled, the old infamy will pop out into daylight like a toad out of a fissure in the rock, and the shadow of the shade of what was once a man will be heartily pilloried by his descendants. A little while ago and Villon was almost totally forgotten; then he was revived for the sake of his verses; and now he is being revived with a vengeance in the detection of his misdemeanors. How unsubstantial is this projection of a man's existence, which can lie in abeyance for centuries and then be brushed up again and set forth for the consideration of posterity by a few dips in an antiquary's inkpot! This precarious tenure of fame goes a long way to justify those (and they are not few) who prefer cakes and cream in the immediate present.

A WILD YOUTH

FRANÇOIS DE MONTCORBIER, *alias* François des Loges, *alias* François Villon, *alias* Michel Mouton, Master of Arts in the University of Paris, was born in that city in the summer of 1431. It was a memorable year for France on other and higher considerations. A great-hearted girl and a poor-hearted boy made, the one her last, the other his first appearance on the public stage of that unhappy country. On the 30th of May the ashes of Joan of Arc were thrown into the Seine, and on the 2d of December our Henry Sixth made his Joyous Entry dismally enough into disaffected and depopulating Paris. Sword and fire still ravaged the open country. On a single April Saturday twelve hundred persons, besides children, made their escape out of the starving capital. The hangman, as is not uninteresting to note in connection with Master Francis, was kept hard at work in 1431; on the last of April and on the 4th of May alone, sixty-two bandits swung from Paris gibbets.

A more confused or troublous time it would have been difficult to select for a start in life. Not even a man's nationality was certain; for the people of Paris there was no such thing as a Frenchman. The English were the English indeed, but the French were only the Armagnacs, whom, with Joan of Arc at their head, they had beaten back from under their ramparts not two years before. Such public sentiment as they had centered about their dear Duke of Burgundy, and the dear Duke had no more urgent business than to keep out of their neighborhood. . . . At least, and whether he liked it or not, our disreputable troubadour was tubbed and swaddled as a subject of the English crown.

We hear nothing of Villon's father except that he was poor and of mean extraction. His mother was given piously, which does not imply very much in an old Frenchwoman, and quite uneducated. He had an uncle, a monk in an abbey at Angers, who must have prospered beyond the family average, and was reported to be worth five or six hundred crowns. Of this uncle and his money-box the reader will hear once more.

In 1448 Francis became a student of the University of Paris; in 1450 he took the degree of Bachelor, and in 1452 that of Master of Arts. His *bourse*, or the sum paid weekly for his board, was of the amount of two sous. Now two sous was about the price of a pound of salt butter in the bad times of 1417; it was the price of half-a-pound in the worse times of 1419; and in 1444, just four years before Villon joined the University, it seems to have been taken as the average wage for a day's manual labor. In short, it cannot have been a very profuse allowance to keep a sharp-set lad in breakfast and supper for seven mortal days; and Villon's share of the cakes and pastry and general good cheer, to which he is never weary of referring, must have been slender from the first.

The educational arrangements of the University of Paris were, to our way of thinking, somewhat incomplete. Worldly and monkish elements were presented in a curious confusion, which the youth might disentangle for himself. If he had an opportunity, on the one hand, of acquiring much hair-drawn divinity and a taste for formal disputation, he was put in the way of much gross and flaunting vice upon the other. The lecture room of a scholastic doctor was sometimes under the same roof with establishments of a very different and peculiarly unedifying order. The students had extraordinary privileges, which by all accounts they abused extraordinarily. And while some condemned themselves to an almost sepulchral regularity and seclusion, others fled the schools, swaggered in the street "with their thumbs in their girdle," passed the night in riot, and behaved themselves as the worthy forerunners of Claude Frollo in the romance of *Notre Dame de Paris*.

Villon tells us himself that he was among the truants, but we hardly needed his avowal. The burlesque erudition in which he sometimes indulged implies no more than the merest smattering of knowledge; whereas his acquaintance with blackguard haunts and industries could only have been acquired by early and consistent impiety and idleness. He passed his degrees, it is true; but some of us who have been to modern universities will make their own reflections on the value of the test. As for his three pupils, Colin Laurent, Girard Gossouyn, and Jehan Marceau— if they were really his pupils in any serious sense—what can we say but God help them! And sure enough, by his own description, they turned out as ragged, rowdy, and ignorant as was to be looked for from the views and manners of their rare preceptor.

At some time or other, before or during his university career, the poet was adopted by Master Guillaume de Villon, chaplain of Saint Benoît-le-Betourne near the Sorbonne. From him he borrowed the surname by which he is known to posterity. It was most likely from his house, called the *Porte Rouge*, and situated in a garden in the cloister of St. Benoît, that Master Francis heard the bell of the Sorbonne ring out the Angelus while he was finishing his *Small Testament* at Christmastide in 1456.

Toward this benefactor he usually gets credit for a respectable display of gratitude. But with his trap and pitfall style of writing, it is easy to make too sure. His sentiments are about as much to be relied on as those of a professional beggar; and in this, as in so many other matters, he comes toward us whining and piping the eye, and goes off again with a whoop and his finger to his nose. Thus, he calls Guillaume de Villon his "more than father," thanks him with a great show of sincerity for having helped him out of many scrapes, and bequeaths him his portion of renown. But the portion of renown which belonged to a young thief, distinguished (if, at the period when he wrote this legacy, he was distinguished at all) for having written some more or less obscene and scurrilous ballads, must have been little fitted to gratify the self-respect or increase the reputation of a benevolent ecclesiastic. The same remark applies to a subsequent legacy of the poet's library, with specification of one work which was plainly neither decent nor devout.

We are thus left on the horns of a dilemma. If the chaplain was a godly, philanthropic personage, who had tried to graft good principles and good behavior on this wild slip of an adopted son, these jesting legacies would obviously cut him to the heart. The position of an adopted son toward his adoptive father is one full of delicacy; where a man lends his name he looks for great consideration. And this legacy of Villon's portion of renown may be taken as the mere fling of an unregenerate scapegrace who has wit enough to recognize in his own shame the readiest weapon of offense against a prosy benefactor's feelings. The gratitude of Master Francis figures, on this reading, as a frightful *minus* quantity. If, on the other hand, those jests were given and taken in good humor, the whole relation between the pair degenerates into the unedifying complicity of a debauched old chaplain and a witty and dissolute young scholar. At this rate the house with the red door may have rung with the most mundane minstrelsy; and it may have been below its roof that Villon, through a hole in the plaster, studied, as he tells us, the leisures of a rich ecclesiastic.

It was, perhaps, of some moment in the poet's life that he should have inhabited the cloister of Saint Benoît. Three of the most remarkable among his early acquaintances are Catherine de Vausselles, for whom he entertained a short-lived affection and an enduring and most unmanly resentment; Regnier de Montigny, a young blackguard of good birth; and Colin de Cayeux, a fellow with a marked aptitude for picking locks. Now we are on a foundation of mere conjecture, but it is at least curious to find that two of the canons of Saint Benoît answered respectively to the names of Pierre de Vaucel and Etienne de Montigny, and that there was a householder called Nicolas de Cayeux in a street—the Rue des Poirées— in the immediate neighborhood of the cloister. M. Longnon is almost ready to identify Catherine as the niece of Pierre, Regnier as the nephew of Etienne, and Colin as the son of Nicolas. Without going so far, it must be owned that the approximation of names is significant. As we go on to see the part played by each of these persons in the sordid melodrama of the poet's life, we shall come to regard it as even more notable. Is it not Clough who has remarked that, after all, everything lies in juxtaposition? Many a man's destiny has been settled by nothing apparently more grave than a pretty face on the opposite side of the street and a couple of bad companions round the corner.

Catherine de Vausselles (or de Vaucel—the change is within the limits of Villon's license) had plainly delighted in the poet's conversation; near neighbors or not, they were much together; and Villon made no secret of his court, and suffered himself to believe that his feeling was repaid in kind. This may have been an error from the first, or he may have estranged her by subsequent misconduct or temerity. One can easily imagine Villon an impatient wooer. One thing, at least, is sure: that the affair terminated in a manner bitterly humiliating to Master Francis. In presence of his lady-love, perhaps under her window and certainly with her connivance, he was unmercifully thrashed by one Noë le Joly—beaten, as he says himself, like dirty linen on the washing-board. It is characteristic that his malice had notably increased between the time when he wrote *The Small Testament* immediately on the back of the occurrence, and the time when he wrote *The Large Testament* five years after. On the latter occasion nothing is too bad for his "damsel with the twisted nose," as he calls her. She is spared neither hint nor accusation, and he tells his messenger to accost her with the vilest insults. Villon, it is thought, was out of Paris when these amenities escaped his pen; or perhaps the strong arm of Noë le Joly would have been again in requisition. So ends the love story, if love story it may properly be called. Poets are not necessarily fortunate in love; but they usually fall among more romantic circumstances and bear their disappointment with a better grace.

The neighborhood of Regnier de Montigny and Colin de Cayeux was probably more influential on his after-life than the contempt of Catherine. For a man who is greedy of all pleasures, and provided with little money and less dignity of character, we may prophesy a safe and speedy voyage downward. Humble or even truckling virtue may walk unspotted in this life. But only those who despise the pleasures can afford to despise the opinion of the world. A man of a strong, heady temperament, like Villon, is very differently tempted. His eyes lay hold on all provocations greedily, and his heart flames up at a look into imperious desire; he is snared and broached-to by anything and everything from a pretty face to a piece of pastry in a cookshop window; he will drink the rinsing of the wine cup, stay the latest at the tavern party, tap at the lighted windows, follow the sound of singing, and beat the whole neighborhood for another reveler, as he goes reluctantly homeward; and grudge himself every hour of sleep as a black empty period in which he cannot follow after pleasure. Such a person is lost if he have not dignity, or, failing that, at least pride, which is its shadow and in many ways its substitute.

Master Francis, I fancy, would follow his own eager instincts without much spiritual struggle. And we soon find him fallen among thieves in sober, literal earnest, and counting as acquaintances the most disreputable people he could lay his hands on: fellows who stole ducks in Paris Moat; sergeants of the criminal court, and archers of the watch; blackguards who slept at night under the butchers' stalls, and for whom the aforesaid archers peered about carefully with lanterns; Regnier de Montigny, Colin de Cayeux, and their crew, all bound on a favoring breeze toward the gallows; the disorderly abbess of Port Royal, who went about at fair time with soldiers and thieves, and conducted her abbey on the queerest principles; and most likely Perette Mauger, the great Paris receiver of stolen goods, not yet dreaming, poor woman! of the last scene of her career when Henry Cousin, executor of the high justice, shall bury her, alive and most reluctant, in front of the new Montigny gibbet.

Nay, our friend soon began to take a foremost rank in this society. He could string off verses, which is always an agreeable talent; and he could make himself useful in many other ways. The whole ragged army of Bohemia, and whosoever loved good cheer without at all loving to work and pay for it, are addressed in contemporary verses as the "Subjects of François Villon." He was a good genius to all hungry and unscrupulous persons; and became the hero of a whole legendary cycle of tavern tricks and cheateries. At best, these were doubtful levities, rather too thievish for a schoolboy, rather too gamesome for a thief. But he would not linger long in this equivocal border land. He must soon have complied with his surroundings. He was one who would go where the cannikin clinked, not caring who should pay; and from supping in the wolves' den, there is but a step to hunting with the pack.

And here, as I am on the chapter of his degradation, I shall say all I mean to say about its darkest expression, and be done with it for good. Some charitable critics see no more than a *jeu d'esprit*, a graceful and trifling exercise of the imagination, in the grimy ballad of Muckle Meg ("Grosse Margot").* I am not able to follow these gentlemen to this

* Page 83.

polite extreme. Out of all Villon's works that ballad stands forth in flaring reality, gross and ghastly, as a thing written in a contraction of disgust. M. Longnon shows us more and more clearly at every page that we are to read our poet literally, that his names are the names of real persons, and the events he chronicles were actual events. But even if the tendency of criticism had run the other way, this ballad would have gone far to prove itself. I can well understand the reluctance of worthy persons in this matter; for of course it is unpleasant to think of a man of genius as one who held, in the words of Marina to Boult:*

> "A place, for which the pained'st fiend
> Of hell would not in reputation change."

But beyond this natural unwillingness, the whole difficulty of the case springs from a highly virtuous ignorance of life. Paris now is not so different from the Paris of then; and the whole of the doings of Bohemia are not written in the sugar-candy pastorals of Murger. It is really not at all surprising that a young man of the fifteenth century, with a knack of making verses, should accept his bread upon disgraceful terms. The race of those who do is not extinct; and some of them to this day write the prettiest verses imaginable. . . . After this, it were impossible for Master Francis to fall lower: to go and steal for himself would be an admirable advance from every point of view, divine or human.

And yet it is not as a thief, but as a homicide, that he makes his first appearance before angry justice. On June 5, 1455, when he was about twenty-four, and had been Master of Arts for a matter of three years, we behold him for the first time quite definitely. Angry justice had, as it were, photographed him in the act of his homicide; and M. Longnon, rummaging among old deeds, has turned up the negative and printed it off for our instruction.

Villon had been supping—copiously we may believe—and sat on a stone bench in front of the Church of St. Benoît, in company with a priest called Gilles and a woman of the name of Isabeau. It was nine o'clock, a mighty late hour for the period, and evidently a fine summer's night. Master Francis carried a mantle, like a prudent man, to keep him

---

* In Shakespeare's *Pericles*.

from the dews (*serain*), and had a sword below it dangling from his girdle. So these three dallied in front of St. Benoît, taking their pleasure (*pour soy esbatre*). Suddenly there arrived upon the scene a priest, Philippe Chermoye or Sermaise, also with sword and cloak, and accompanied by one Master Jehan le Mardi. Sermaise, according to Villon's account, which is all we have to go upon, came up blustering and denying God; as Villon rose to make room for him upon the bench, thrust him rudely back into his place; and finally drew his sword and cut open his lower lip, by what I should imagine was a very clumsy stroke.

Up to this point, Villon professes to have been a model of courtesy, even of feebleness: and the brawl, in his version, reads like the fable of the wolf and the lamb. But now the lamb was roused; he drew his sword, stabbed Sermaise in the groin, knocked him on the head with a big stone, and then, leaving him to his fate, went away to have his own lip doctored by a barber of the name of Fouquet. In one version, he says that Gilles, Isabeau, and Le Mardi ran away at the first high words, and that he and Sermaise had it out alone; in another, Le Mardi is represented as returning and wresting Villon's sword from him: the reader may please himself. Sermaise was picked up, lay all that night in the prison of Saint Benoît, where he was examined by an official of the Châtelet and expressly pardoned Villon, and died on the following Saturday in the Hôtel Dieu.

This, as I have said, was in June. Not before January of the next year could Villon extract a pardon from the king; but while his hand was in, he got two. One is for "François des Loges, alias (*autrement dit*) de Villon"; and the other runs in the name of François de Montcorbier. Nay, it appears there was a further complication; for in the narrative of the first of these documents, it is mentioned that he passed himself off upon Fouquet, the barber-surgeon, as one Michel Mouton.

M. Longnon has a theory that this unhappy accident with Sermaise was the cause of Villon's subsequent irregularities; and that up to that moment he had been the pink of good behavior. But the matter has to my eyes a more dubious air. A pardon necessary for Des Loges and another for Montcorbier? and these two the same person? and one or both of them known by the *alias* of Villon, however honestly come by? and lastly, in the heat of the moment, a fourth name thrown out with an assured countenance? A ship is not to be trusted that sails under so many colors.

This is not the simple bearing of innocence. No—the young master was already treading crooked paths; already, he would start and blench at a hand upon his shoulder, with the look we know so well in the face of Hogarth's Idle Apprentice; already, in the blue devils, he would see Henry Cousin, the executor of high justice, going in dolorous procession toward Montfaucon, and hear the wind and the birds crying around Paris gibbet.

A GANG OF THIEVES

IN SPITE OF the prodigious number of people who managed to get hanged, the fifteenth century was by no means a bad time for criminals. A great confusion of parties and great dust of fighting favored the escape of private housebreakers and quiet fellows who stole ducks in Paris Moat. Prisons were leaky; and as we shall see, a man with a few crowns in his pocket—and perhaps some acquaintance among the officials—could easily slip out and become once more a free marauder. There was no want of a sanctuary where he might harbor until troubles blew by; and accomplices helped each other with more or less good faith.

Clerks, above all, had remarkable facilities for a criminal way of life; for they were privileged, except in cases of notorious incorrigibility, to be plucked from the hands of rude secular justice and tried by a tribunal of their own. In 1402, a couple of thieves, both clerks of the University, were condemned to death by the Provost of Paris. As they were taken to Montfaucon, they kept crying "high and clearly" for their benefit of clergy, but were nonetheless pitilessly hanged and gibbeted. Indignant Alma Mater interfered before the king; and the Provost was deprived of all royal offices, and condemned to return the bodies and erect a great stone cross, on the road from Paris to the gibbet, graven with the effigies of these two holy martyrs.

We shall hear more of the benefit of clergy; for after this the reader will not be surprised to meet with thieves in the shape of tonsured clerks, or even priests and monks.

To a knot of such learned pilferers our poet certainly belonged; and by turning over a few more of M. Longnon's negatives, we shall get a clear idea of their character and doings. Montigny and De Cayeux are names already known; Guy Tabary, Petit-Jehan, Dom Nicolas, little Thibault, who was both clerk and goldsmith, and who made picklocks and melted plate for himself and his companions—with these the reader has still to become acquainted. Petit-Jehan and De Cayeux were handy fellows and enjoyed a useful pre-eminence in honor of their doings with the picklock. But the flower of the flock was little Thibault; it was reported that no lock could stand before him; he had a persuasive hand; let us salute capacity wherever we may find it.

Perhaps the term *gang* is not quite properly applied to the persons whose fortunes we are now about to follow; rather they were independent malefactors, socially intimate, and occasionally joining together for some serious operation, just as modern stockjobbers form a syndicate for an important loan. Nor were they at all particular to any branch of misdoing. They did not scrupulously confine themselves to a single sort of theft, as I hear is common among modern thieves. They were ready for anything, from pitch-and-toss to manslaughter. Montigny, for instance, had neglected neither of these extremes, and we find him accused of cheating at games of hazard on the one hand and on the other of the murder of one Thevenin Pensete in a house by the Cemetery of St. John. If time had only spared us some particulars, might not this last have furnished us with the matter of a grisly winter's tale?

At Christmas-time in 1456, readers of Villon will remember that he was engaged on *The Small Testament*. About the same period, *circa festum nativitatis Domini*, he took part in a memorable supper at the Mule Tavern, in front of the Church of St. Mathurin. Tabary, who seems to have been very much Villon's creature, had ordered the supper in the course of the afternoon. He was a man who had had troubles in his time and languished in the Bishop of Paris's prisons on a suspicion of picking locks—confiding, convivial, not very astute—who had copied out a whole improper romance with his own right hand. This supper-party was to be his first introduction to De Cayeux and Petit-Jehan, which was probably a matter of some concern to the poor man's muddy wits; in the sequel, at least, he speaks of both with an undisguised respect, based on professional inferiority in the matter of picklocks. Dom Nicolas, a Picardy monk, was the fifth and last at table.

When supper had been dispatched and fairly washed down, we may suppose, with white Baigneux or red Beaune, which were favorite wines among the fellowship, Tabary was solemnly sworn over to secrecy on the night's performances; and the party left the Mule and proceeded to an unoccupied house belonging to Robert de Saint-Simon. This, over a low wall, they entered without difficulty. All but Tabary took off their upper garments; a ladder was found and applied to the high wall which separated Saint-Simon's house from the court of the College of Navarre; the four fellows in their shirt-sleeves (as we might say) clambered over in a twinkling; and Master Guy Tabary remained alone beside the overcoats.

From the court the burglars made their way into the vestry of the chapel, where they found a large chest, strengthened with iron bands and closed with four locks. One of these locks they picked, and then, by levering up the corner, forced the other three. Inside was a small coffer, of walnut wood, also barred with iron, but fastened with only three locks, which were all comfortably picked by way of the keyhole. In the walnut coffer—a joyous sight by our thieves' lantern—were five hundred crowns of gold. There was some talk of opening the aumries,* where, if they had only known, a booty eight or nine times greater lay ready to their hand; but one of the party (I have a humorous suspicion it was Dom Nicolas, the Picardy monk) hurried them away. It was ten o'clock when they mounted the ladder; it was about midnight before Tabary beheld them coming back. To him they gave ten crowns, and promised a share of a two-crown dinner on the morrow; whereat we may suppose his mouth watered. In course of time, he got wind of the real amount of their booty and understood how scurvily he had been used; but he seems to have borne no malice. How could he, against such superb operators as Petit-Jehan and De Cayeux; or a person like Villon, who could have made a new improper romance out of his own head, instead of merely copying an old one with mechanical right hand?

The rest of the winter was not uneventful for the gang. First they made a demonstration against the Church of St. Mathurin after chalices, and were ignominiously chased away by barking dogs. Then Tabary fell out with Casin Chollet, one of the fellows who stole ducks in Paris Moat,

* Repositories.

who subsequently became a sergeant of the Châtelet and distinguished himself by misconduct, followed by imprisonment and public castigation, during the wars of Louis Eleventh. The quarrel was not conducted with a proper regard to the king's peace, and the pair publicly belabored each other until the police stepped in, and Master Tabary was cast once more into the prisons of the Bishop.

While he still lay in durance, another job was cleverly executed by the band in broad daylight, at the Augustine Monastery. Brother Guillaume Coiffier was beguiled by an accomplice to St. Mathurin to say mass; and during his absence, his chamber was entered and five or six hundred crowns in money and some silver plate successfully abstracted. A melancholy man was Coiffier on his return! Eight crowns from this adventure were forwarded by little Thibault to the incarcerated Tabary; and with these he bribed the jailer and reappeared in Paris taverns.

Some time before or shortly after this, Villon set out for Angers, as he had promised in *The Small Testament*. The object of this excursion was not merely to avoid the presence of his cruel mistress or the strong arm of Noë le Joly, but to plan a deliberate robbery on his uncle the monk. As soon as he had properly studied the ground, the others were to go over in force from Paris—picklocks and all—and away with my uncle's strong-box!

This throws a comical sidelight on his own accusation against his relatives, that they had "forgotten natural duty" and disowned him because he was poor. A poor relation is a distasteful circumstance at the best, but a poor relation who plans deliberate robberies against those of his blood, and trudges hundreds of weary leagues to put them into execution, is surely a little on the wrong side of toleration. The uncle at Angers may have been monstrously undutiful; but the nephew from Paris was upsides with him.

On the 23d April, that venerable and discreet person, Master Pierre Marchand, Curate and Prior of Paray-le-Monial, in the diocese of Chartres, arrived in Paris and put up at the sign of the Three Chandeliers, in the Rue de la Huchette. Next day, or the day after, as he was breakfasting at the sign of the Armchair, he fell into talk with two customers, one of whom was a priest and the other our friend Tabary. The idiotic Tabary became mighty confidential as to his past life. Pierre Marchand, who was an acquaintance of Guillaume Coiffier's and had sympathized with him over his loss, pricked up his ears at the mention of picklocks, and led on the transcriber of improper romances from one thing to another, until they were fast friends. For picklocks the Prior of Paray professed a keen curiosity; but Tabary, upon some late alarm, had thrown all his into the Seine. Let that be no difficulty, however, for was there not little Thibault, who could make them of all shapes and sizes, and to whom Tabary, smelling an accomplice, would be only too glad to introduce his new acquaintance?

On the morrow, accordingly, they met; and Tabary, after having first wet his whistle at the Prior's expense, led him to Notre Dame and presented him to four or five "young companions," who were keeping sanctuary in the church. They were all clerks, recently escaped, like Tabary himself, from the episcopal prisons. Among these we may notice Thibault, the operator, a little fellow of twenty-six, wearing long hair behind. The Prior expressed, through Tabary, his anxiety to become their accomplice and altogether such as they were. Mighty polite they showed themselves, and made him many fine speeches in return. But for all that, perhaps because they had longer heads than Tabary, perhaps because it is less easy to wheedle men in a body, they kept obstinately to generalities and gave him no information as to their exploits, past, present, or to come. I suppose Tabary groaned under this reserve; for no sooner were he and the Prior out of the church than he fairly emptied his heart to him, gave him full details of many hanging matters in the past, and explained the future intentions of the band. The scheme of the hour was to rob another Augustine monk, Robert de la Porte, and in this the Prior agreed to take a hand with simulated greed. Thus, in the course of two days, he had turned this wineskin of a Tabary inside out.

For a while longer the farce was carried on; the Prior was introduced to Petit-Jehan, whom he describes as a little, very smart man of thirty, with a black beard and a short jacket; an appointment was made and broken in the de la Porte affair; Tabary had some breakfast at the Prior's charge and leaked out more secrets under the influence of wine and friendship; and then all of a sudden, on the 17th of May, an alarm sprang up, the Prior picked up his skirts and walked quietly over to the Châtelet to make a deposition, and the whole band took to their heels and vanished out of Paris and the sight of the police.

Vanish as they like, they all go with a clog about their feet. Sooner or later, here or there, they will be caught in the fact, and ignominiously sent home. From our vantage of four centuries afterward, it is odd and pitiful to watch the order in which the fugitives are captured and dragged in.

Montigny was the first. In August of that same year, he was laid by the heels on many grievous counts: sacrilegious robberies, frauds, incorrigibility, and that bad business about Thevenin Pensete in the house by the Cemetery of St. John. He was reclaimed by the ecclesiastical authorities as a clerk; but the claim was rebutted on the score of incorrigibility, and ultimately fell to the ground; and he was condemned to death by the Provost of Paris. It was a very rude hour for Montigny, but hope was not yet over. He was a fellow of some birth; his father had been king's pantler;* his sister, probably married to someone about the Court, was in the family way, and her health would be endangered if the execution was proceeded with. So down comes Charles Seventh with the letters of mercy, commuting the penalty to a year in a dungeon on bread and water, and a pilgrimage to the shrine of St. James in Galicia.

Alas! the document was incomplete; it did not contain the full tale of Montigny's enormities; it did not recite that he had been denied benefit of clergy, and it said nothing about Thevenin Pensete. Montigny's hour was at hand. Benefit of clergy, honorable descent from king's pantler, sister in the family way, royal letters of commutation—all were of no avail. He had been in prison in Rouen, in Tours, in Bordeaux, and four times already in Paris; and out of all these he had come scatheless; but now he must make a little excursion as far as Montfaucon with Henry Cousin, executor of high justice. There let him swing among the carrion crows.

About a year later, in July 1458, the police laid hands on Tabary. Before the ecclesiastical commissary he was twice examined, and, on the latter occasion, put to the question ordinary and extraordinary. What a dismal change from pleasant suppers at the Mule, where he sat in triumph with expert operators and great wits! He is at the lees of life, poor rogue; and those fingers which once transcribed improper romances are now agonizingly stretched upon the rack. We have no sure knowledge, but we may have a shrewd guess of the conclusion. Tabary, the admirer, would go the same way as those whom he admired.

* Officer in charge of the pantry.

The last we hear of is Colin de Cayeux. He was caught in autumn 1460, in the great Church of St. Leu d'Esserens, which makes so fine a figure in the pleasant Oise Valley between Creil and Beaumont. He was reclaimed by no less than two bishops; but the Procureur for the Provost held fast by incorrigible Colin. Fourteen hundred sixty was an ill-starred year: for justice was making a clean sweep of "poor and indigent persons, thieves, cheats, and lockpickers," in the neighborhood of Paris; and Colin de Cayeux, with many others, was condemned to death and hanged.

VILLON AND THE GALLOWS

VILLON WAS STILL ABSENT on the Angers expedition when the Prior of Paray sent such a bombshell among his accomplices; and the dates of his return and arrest remain undiscoverable. M. Campaux plausibly enough opined for the autumn of 1457, which would make him closely follow on Montigny, and the first of those denounced by the Prior to fall into the toils. We may suppose, at least, that it was not long thereafter; we may suppose him competed for between lay and clerical Courts; and we may suppose him alternately pert and impudent, humble and fawning, in his defense.

But at the end of all supposing, we come upon some nuggets of fact. For first, he was put to the question by water. He who had tossed off so many cups of white Baigneux or red Beaune, now drank water through linen folds, until his bowels were flooded and his heart stood still. After so much raising of the elbow, so much outcry of fictitious thirst, here at last was enough drinking for a lifetime. Truly, of our pleasant vices, the gods make whips to scourge us. And secondly he was condemned to be hanged.

A man may have been expecting a catastrophe for years, and yet find himself unprepared when it arrives. Certainly, Villon found, in this legitimate issue of his career, a very staggering and grave consideration. Every beast, as he says, clings bitterly to a whole skin. If everything is lost, and even honor, life still remains; nay, and it becomes, like the ewe lamb in Nathan's parable, as dear as all the rest.

"Do you fancy," he asks, in a lively ballad, "that I had not enough philosophy under my hood to cry out: 'I appeal'? If I had made any bones about the matter, I should have been planted upright in the fields, by the St. Denis Road"—Montfaucon being on the way to St. Denis. An appeal to Parliament, as we saw in the case of Colin de Cayeux, did not necessarily lead to an acquittal or a commutation; amd while the matter was pending, our poet had ample opportunity to reflect on his position. Hanging is a sharp argument, and to swing with many others on the gibbet adds a horrible corollary for the imagination. With the aspect of Montfaucon he was well acquainted; indeed, as the neighborhood appears to have been sacred to junketing and nocturnal picnics of wild young men and women, he had probably studied it under all varieties of hour and weather. And now, as he lay in prison waiting the mortal push, these different aspects crowded back on his imagination with a new and startling significance; and he wrote a ballad, by way of epitaph for himself and his companions, which remains unique in the annals of mankind. It is, in the highest sense, a piece of his biography :

> *La pluye nous a debuez et lavez,*
> *Et le soleil dessechez et noirciz;*
> *Pies, corbeaulx, nous ont les yeux cavez,*
> *Et arrachez la barbe et les sourcilz.*
> *Jamais, nul temps, nous ne sommes assis;*
> *Puis çà, puis là, comme le vent varie,*
> *A son plaisir sans cesser nous charie,*
> *Plus becquetez d'oiseaulx que dez à couldre.*
> *Ne soyez donc de nostre confrairie,*
> *Mais priez Dieu que tous nous vueille absouldre.**

Here is some genuine thieves' literature after so much that was spurious; sharp as an etching, written with a shuddering soul. There is an intensity of consideration in the piece that shows it to be the transcript of familiar thoughts. It is the quintessence of many a doleful nightmare on the straw, when he felt himself swing helpless in the wind, and saw the birds turn about him, screaming and menacing his eyes.

* For a translation, see third stanza of "The Epitaph in Form of a Ballad," page 119.

And, after all, the Parliament changed his sentence into one of banishment; and to Roussillon, in Dauphiny, our poet must carry his woes without delay. Travelers between Lyons and Marseilles may remember a station on the line, some way below Vienne, where the Rhone fleets seaward between vine-clad hills. This was Villon's Siberia. It would be a little warm in summer perhaps, and a little cold in winter in that draughty valley between two great mountain fields; but what with the hills, and the racing river, and the fiery Rhone wines, he was little to be pitied on the conditions of his exile. Villon, in a remarkably bad ballad, written in a breath, heartily thanked and fulsomely belauded the Parliament: the *envoi*, like the proverbial postscript of a lady's letter, containing the pith of his performance in a request for three days' delay to settle his affairs and bid his friends farewell.

He was probably not followed out of Paris, like Antoine Fradin, the popular preacher, another exile of a few years later, by weeping multitudes; but I daresay one or two rogues of his acquaintance would keep him company for a mile or so on the south road, and drink a bottle with him before they turned. For banished people, in those days, seem to have set out on their own responsibility, in their own guard, and at their own expense. It was no joke to make one's way from Paris to Roussillon alone and penniless in the fifteenth century. Villon says he left a rag of his tails on every bush. Indeed, he must have had many a weary tramp, many a slender meal, and many a to-do with blustering captains of the Ordonnance. But with one of his light fingers, we may fancy that he took as good as he gave; for every rag of his tail, he would manage to indemnify himself upon the population in the shape of food, or wine, or ringing money; and his route would be traceable across France and Burgundy by housewives and innkeepers lamenting over petty thefts, like the track of a single human locust.

A strange figure he must have cut in the eyes of the good country people: this ragged, blackguard city poet, with a smack of the Paris student, and a smack of the Paris street arab, posting along the highways, in rain or sun, among the green fields and vineyards. For himself, he had no taste for rural loveliness; green fields and vineyards would be mighty indifferent to Master Francis; but he would often have his tongue in his cheek at the simplicity of rustic dupes, and often, at city gates, he might stop to contemplate the gibbet with its swinging bodies, and hug himself on his escape.

How long he stayed at Roussillon, how far he became the protégé of the Bourbons, to whom that town belonged, or when it was that he took part, under the auspices of Charles of Orleans, in a rhyming tournament to be referred to once again in the pages of the present volume, are matters that still remain in darkness, in spite of M. Longnon's diligent rummaging among archives.

When we next find him, in summer 1461, alas! he is once more in durance: this time at Meung-sur-Loire, in the prisons of Thibault d'Aussigny, Bishop of Orleans. He had been lowered in a basket into a noisome pit, where he lay, all summer, gnawing hard crusts and railing upon fate. His teeth, he says, were like the teeth of a rake: a touch of haggard portraiture all the more real for being excessive and burlesque, and all the more proper to the man for being a caricature of his own misery. His eyes were "bandaged with thick walls." It might blow hurricanes overhead; the lightning might leap in high heaven; but no word of all this reached him in his noisome pit. *"Il n'entre, ou gist, n'escler ni tourbillon."* * Above all, he was fevered with envy and anger at the freedom of others; and his heart flowed over into curses as he thought of Thibault d'Aussigny, walking the streets in God's sunlight, and blessing people with extended fingers. So much we find sharply lined in his own poems. Why he was cast again into prison—how he had again managed to shave the gallows—this we know not, nor, from the destruction of authorities, are we ever likely to learn. But on October 2, 1461, or some day immediately preceding, the new king, Louis Eleventh, made his joyous entry into Meung. Now it was a part of the formality on such occasions for the new king to liberate certain prisoners; and so the basket was let down into Villon's pit, and hastily did Master Francis scramble in, and was most joyfully hauled up, and shot out, blinking and tottering, but once more a free man, into the blessed sun and wind.

Now or never is the time for verses! Such a happy revolution would turn the head of a stocking-weaver, and set him jingling rhymes. And so—after a voyage to Paris, where he finds Montigny and De Cayeux

* See second stanza of "Epistle in Form of a Ballad to His Friends," page 115.

clattering their bones upon the gibbet, and his three pupils roistering in Paris streets, "with their thumbs under their girdles"—down sits Master Francis to write his *Large Testament*, and perpetuate his name in a sort of glorious ignominy.

THE LARGE TESTAMENT

OF THIS CAPITAL ACHIEVEMENT and, with it, of Villon's style in general, it is here the place to speak. *The Large Testament* is a hurly-burly of cynical and sentimental reflections about life, jesting legacies to friends and enemies, and, interspersed among these, many admirable ballades, both serious and absurd. With so free a design, no thought that occurred to him would need to be dismissed without expression; and he could draw at full length the portrait of his own bedeviled soul, and of the bleak and blackguardly world which was the theater of his exploits and sufferings. If the reader can conceive something between the slap-dash inconsequence of Byron's *Don Juan* and the racy humorous gravity and brief noble touches that distinguish the vernacular poems of Burns, he will have formed some idea of Villon's style.

To the latter writer—except in the ballades, which are quite his own, and can be paralleled from no other language known to me—he bears a particular resemblance. In common with Burns he has a certain rugged compression, a brutal vivacity of epithet, a homely vigor, a delight in local personalities, and an interest in many sides of life, that are often despised and passed over by more effete and cultured poets. Both also, in their strong, easy colloquial way, tend to become difficult and obscure, the obscurity in the case of Villon passing at times into the absolute darkness of cant language. They are perhaps the only two great masters of expression who keep sending their readers to a glossary.

"Shall we not dare to say of a thief," asks Montaigne, "that he has a handsome leg?" It is a far more serious claim that we have to put forward in behalf of Villon. Beside that of his contemporaries, his writing, so full of color, so eloquent, so picturesque, stands out in an almost miraculous isolation. If only one or two of the chroniclers could have taken a leaf out of his book, history would have been a pastime, and the fifteenth century as present to our minds as the age of Charles Second. This gallow's-bird was the one great writer of his age and country, and initiated modern literature for France. Boileau, long ago, in the period of perukes and snuff-boxes, recognized him as the first articulate poet in the language; and if we measure him, not by priority of merit, but living duration of influence—not on a comparison with obscure forerunners, but with great and famous successors—we shall install this ragged and disreputable figure in a far higher niche in glory's temple than was ever dreamed of by the critic.

It is, in itself, a memorable fact that, before 1542, in the very dawn of printing, and while modern France was in the making, the works of Villon ran through seven different editions. Out of him flows much of Rabelais; and through Rabelais, directly and indirectly, a deep, permanent, and growing inspiration. Not only his style but his callous pertinent way of looking upon the sordid and ugly sides of life becomes every day a more specific feature in the literature of France. And only the other year, a work of some power appeared in Paris, and appeared with infinite scandal, which owed its whole inner significance and much of its outward form to the study of our rhyming thief.

The world to which he introduces us is, as before said, blackguardly and bleak. Paris swarms before us, full of famine, shame, and death; monks and the servants of great lords hold high wassail upon cakes and pastry; the poor man licks his lips before the baker's window; people with patched eyes sprawl all night under the stalls; chuckling Tabary transcribes an improper romance; bare-bosomed lasses and ruffling students swagger in the streets; the drunkard goes stumbling homeward; the graveyard is full of bones; and away on Montfaucon, Colin de Cayeux and Montigny hang draggled in the rain. Is there nothing better to be seen than sordid misery and worthless joys? Only where the poor old mother of the poet kneels in church below painted windows, and makes tremulous supplication to the Mother of God.*

In our mixed world, full of green fields and happy lovers, where not long before Joan of Arc had led one of the highest and noblest lives in the

* See "His Mother's Service to Our Lady," page 59.

whole story of mankind, this was all worth chronicling that our poet could perceive. His eyes were indeed sealed with his own filth. He dwelt all his life in a pit more noisome than the dungeon at Meung. In the moral world, also, there are large phenomena not cognizable out of holes and corners. Loud winds blow, speeding home deep-laden ships and sweeping rubbish from the earth; the lightning leaps and cleans the face of heaven; high purposes and brave passions shake and sublimate men's spirits; and meanwhile, in the narrow dungeon of his soul, Villon is mumbling crusts and picking vermin.

Along with this deadly gloom of outlook, we must take another characteristic of his work: its unrivaled insincerity. I can give no better similitude of this quality than I have given already: that he comes up with a whine, and runs away with a whoop and his finger to his nose. His pathos is that of a professional mendicant who should happen to be a man of genius; his levity that of a bitter street arab, full of bread. On a first reading, the pathetic passages preoccupy the reader, and he is cheated out of an alms in the shape of sympathy. But when the thing is studied the illusion fades away: in the transitions, above all, we can detect the evil, ironical temper of the man; and instead of a flighty work, where many crude but genuine feelings tumble together for the mastery as in the lists of tournament, we are tempted to think of *The Large Testament* as of one long-drawn epical grimace, pulled by a merry-andrew, who has found a certain despicable eminence over human respect and human affections by perching himself astride upon the gallows. Between these two views, at best, all temperate judgments will be found to fall; and rather, as I imagine, toward the last.

There were two things on which he felt with perfect and, in one case, even threatening sincerity.

The first of these was an undisguised envy of those richer than himself. He was forever drawing a parallel, already exemplified from his own words, between the happy life of the well-to-do and the miseries of the poor. Burns, too proud and honest not to work, continued through all reverses to sing of poverty with a light, defiant note. Béranger waited till he was himself beyond the reach of want, before writing "The Old Vagabond" or "Jacques." Samuel Johnson, although he was very sorry to be poor, "was a great arguer for the advantages of poverty" in his ill days.

Thus it is that brave men carry their crosses, and smile with the fox burrowing in their vitals.

But Villon, who had not the courage to be poor with honesty, now whiningly implores our sympathy, now shows his teeth upon the dung-heap with an ugly snarl. He envies bitterly, envies passionately. Poverty, he protests, drives men to steal, as hunger makes the wolf sally from the forest. The poor, he goes on, will always have a carping word to say, or, if that outlet be denied, nourish rebellious thoughts. It is a calumny on the noble army of the poor. Thousands in a small way of life, ay, and even in the smallest, go through life with tenfold as much honor and dignity and peace of mind, as the rich gluttons whose dainties and state-beds awakened Villon's covetous temper. And every morning's sun sees thousands who pass whistling to their toil. But Villon was the *"mauvais pauvre"* defined by Victor Hugo, and, in its English expression, so admirably stereotyped by Dickens. He was the first wicked sansculotte. He is the man of genius with the moleskin cap. He is mighty pathetic and beseeching here in the street, but I would not go down a dark road with him for a large consideration.

The second of the points on which he was genuine and emphatic was common to the Middle Ages: a deep and somewhat sniveling conviction of the transitory nature of this life and the pity and horror of death. Old age and the grave, with some dark and yet half-skeptical terror of an after-world—these were ideas that clung about his bones like a disease. An old ape, as he says, may play all the tricks in its repertory, and none of them will tickle an audience into good humor (*Tousjours vieil synge est desplaisant*). It is not the old jester who receives most recognition at a tavern party, but the young fellow, fresh and handsome, who knows the new slang, and carries off his vice with a certain air. Of this, as a tavern jester himself, he would be pointedly conscious. As for the women with whom he was best acquainted, his reflections on their old age, in all their harrowing pathos, shall remain in the original for me. Horace has disgraced himself to something the same tune; but what Horace throws out with an ill-favored laugh, Villon dwells on with an almost maudlin whimper.

It is in death that he finds his truest inspiration, in the swift and sorrowful change that overtakes beauty, in the strange revolution by which great fortunes and renowns are diminished to a handful of church-yard dust, and in the utter passing away of what was once lovable and mighty. It is in this that the mixed texture of his thought enables him to reach such poignant and terrible effects, and to enhance pity with ridi-cule, like a man cutting capers to a funeral march. It is in this, also, that he rises out of himself into the higher spheres of art.

So, in the ballade by which he is best known,* he rings the changes on names that once stood for beautiful and queenly women, and are now no more than letters and a legend. "Where are the snows of yester-year?" runs the burden. And so, in another not so famous,† he passes in review the different degrees of bygone men, for the Holy Apostles and the golden Emperor of the East, down to the heralds, pursuivants, and trumpeters, who also bore their part in the world's pageantries and ate greedily at great folks' tables: all this to the refrain of "So much carry the winds away!"

Probably, there was some melancholy in his mind for a yet lower grade, and Montigny and Colin de Cayeux clattering their bones on Paris gibbet. Alas, and with so pitiful an experience of life, Villon can offer us nothing but terror and lamentation about death! No one has ever more skillfully communicated his own disenchantment; no one ever blown a more ear-piercing note of sadness. This unrepentant thief can attain neither to Christian confidence nor to the spirit of the bright Greek saying: that whom the gods love die early. It is a poor heart, and a poorer age, that cannot accept the conditions of life with some heroic readiness.

꙲ꙫ   ꙲ꙫ   ꙲ꙫ

THE DATE of *The Large Testament* is the last date in the poet's biog-raphy. After having achieved that admirable and despicable performance, he disappears into the night from whence he came. How or when he died, whether decently in bed or trussed up to a gallows, remains a riddle for foolhardy commentators. It appears his health had suffered in the pit at Meung; he was thirty years of age and quite bald; with the notch in his

* "Ballad of Dead Ladies," page 41.
† "Second Ballad of the Lords of Old Time," page 45.

under lip where Sermaise had struck him with the sword, and what wrinkles the reader may imagine.

In default of portraits, this is all I have been able to piece together, and perhaps even the baldness should be taken as a figure of his destitution. A sinister dog, in all likelihood, but with a look in his eye, and the loose flexile mouth that goes with wit and an overweening sensual temperament. Certainly the sorriest figure on the rolls of fame.

A NOTE ON THE TEXT

THE POETRY of François Villon may be divided into three major sections. *Le Petit Testament* (1456) is a series of forty facetious legacies in eight-line stanzas. *Le Grand Testament* (1461), the poem that made him famous, consists chiefly of another 173 eight-line stanzas; in these Villon reviews his life as a beggar and a thief, and in a long series of bequests expresses his melancholy, pathetic, and bitterly humorous views of life. Interspersed in *Le Grand Testament* are his great *ballades* and *rondeaux*. Finally, composed at various times, are the *Poésies Diverses*: more *ballades*, along with other verses.

This collection of translations is confined to Villon's lyrical poems extracted from *Le Grand Testament* and *Poésies Diverses*. The predominating form is the *ballade*, which (as Léonie Adams has remarked) is "the most complex and diversified form of medieval poetry. Villon's *ballades* represent the range of his ability."

Obviously, translation of work of this sort involves a considerable distortion. In the case of Villon's *ballades* another distortion is brought about by removing them from their context. It is hoped that this may in part be alleviated by reading them in conjunction with the introductory essay by Robert Louis Stevenson.

Stevenson's study originally appeared in one of the periodicals to which he contributed. When the piece was reprinted in 1882 in his *Familiar Studies of Men and Books*, he made the following curious comment:

> I am tempted to regret that I ever wrote on this subject, not merely because the paper strikes me as too picturesque by half, but because I regarded Villon as a bad fellow. Others still think well of him, and can find beautiful and human traits where I saw nothing but artistic evil; and by the principle of the art, those should have written of the man, and not I. Where you see no good, silence is the best. Though this penitence comes too late, it may be well, at least, to give it expression.

For the source of much of his material, Stevenson cites Longnon's *Étude Biographique sur François Villon* (Paris, 1877). The footnotes in the essay have been supplied by the editor.

THE POEMS

Dictes moy ou, n'en quel pays,
Est Flora la belle Rommaine,
Archipiades, ne Thaïs,
Qui fut sa cousine germaine,
Écho parlant quant bruyt on maine
Dessus riviere ou sus estan,
Qui beaulté ot trop plus qu'humaine.
Mais ou sont les neiges d'antan?

Ou est la tres sage Helloïs,
Pour qui chastré fut et puis moyne
Pierre Esbaillart a Saint Denis?
Pour son amour ot ceste essoyne.
Semblablement, ou est la royne
Qui commanda que Buridan
Fust geté en ung sac en Saine?
Mais ou sont les neiges d'antan?

La royne Blanche comme lis
Qui chantoit a voix de seraine,
Berte au grant pié, Bietris, Alis,
Haremburgis qui tint le Maine,
Et Jehanne la bonne Lorraine
Qu'Englois brulerent a Rouan;
Ou sont ilz, ou, Vierge souvraine?
Mais ou sont les neiges d'antan?

Prince, n'enquerez de sepmaine
Ou elles sont, ne de cest an,
Qu'a ce reffrain ne vous remaine:
Mais ou sont les neiges d'antan?

BALLAD OF DEAD LADIES

Tell me now in what hidden way is
Lady Flora the lovely Roman?
Where's Hipparchia, and where is Thaïs,
Neither of them the fairer woman?
Where is Echo, beheld of no man,
Only heard on river and mere, –
She whose beauty was more than human? . . .
But where are the snows of yester-year?

Where's Héloise, the learned nun,
For whose sake Abeillard, I ween,
Lost manhood and put priesthood on?
(From Love he won such dule and teen!)
And where, I pray you, is the Queen
Who willed that Buridan should steer
Sewed in a sack's mouth down the Seine? . . .
But where are the snows of yester-year?

White Queen Blanche, like a queen of lilies,
With a voice like any mermaiden, –
Bertha Broadfoot, Beatrice, Alice,
And Ermengarde the lady of Maine, –
And that good Joan whom Englishmen
At Rouen doomed and burned her there, –
Mother of God, where are they then? . . .
But where are the snows of yester-year?

Nay, never ask this week, fair lord,
Where they are gone, nor yet this year,
Save with this much for an overword, –
But where are the snows of yester-year?

Qui plus, ou est le tiers Calixte,
Dernier decedé de ce nom,
Qui quatre ans tint le papaliste?
Alphonce le roy d'Arragon,
Le gracieux duc de Bourbon,
Et Artus le duc de Bretaigne,
Et Charles septiesme le bon?
Mais ou est le preux Charlemaigne?

Semblablement, le roy Scotiste
Qui demy face ot, ce dit on,
Vermeille comme une amatiste
Depuis le front jusqu'au menton?
Le roy de Chippre de renon,
Helas! et le bon roy d'Espaigne
Duquel je ne sçay pas le nom?
Mais ou est le preux Charlemaigne?

D'en plus parler je me desiste;
Le monde n'est qu'abusion.
Il n'est qui contre mort resiste
Ne qui treuve provision.
Encor fais une question:
Lancelot le roy de Behaigne,
Ou est il? Ou est son tayon?
Mais ou est le preux Charlemaigne?

Ou est Claquin le bon Breton?
Ou le conte Daulphin d'Auvergne
Et le bon feu duc d'Alençon?
Mais ou est le preux Charlemaigne?

BALLAD OF THE LORDS OF OLD TIME

What more? Where is the third Calixt,
Last of that name now dead and gone,
Who held four years the Papalist?
Alfonso, king of Aragon,
The gracious lord, duke of Bourbon,
And Arthur, duke of old Britaine?
And Charles the Seventh, that worthy one?
Even with the good knight Charlemain.

The Scot too, king of mount and mist,
With half his face vermilion,
Men tell us, like an amethyst
From brow to chin that blazed and shone;
The Cypriote king of old renown,
Alas! and that good king of Spain,
Whose name I cannot think upon?
Even with the good knight Charlemain.

No more to say of them I list;
'Tis all but vain, all dead and done:
For death may no man born resist,
Nor make appeal when death comes on.
I make yet one more question;
Where's Lancelot, king of far Bohain?
Where's he whose grandson called him son?
Even with the good knight Charlemain.

Where is Guesclin, the good Breton?
The lord of the eastern mountain-chain,
And the good late duke of Alençon?
Even with the good knight Charlemain.

AUTRE BALLADE DES SEIGNEURS
DU TEMPS JADIS

Car, ou soit ly sains apostolles,
D'aubes vestus, d'amys coeffez,
Qui ne saint fors saintes estolles
Dont par le col prent ly mauffez
De mal talant tout eschauffez,
Aussi bein meurt que cilz servans,
De ceste vie cy bouffez:
Autant en emporte ly vens.

Voire, ou soit de Constantinobles
L'emperieres au poing dorez,
Ou de France ly roy tres nobles
Sur tous autres roys decorez,
Qui pour ly grans Dieux aourez
Bastist eglises et couvens,
S'en son temps il fut honnorez,
Autant en emporte ly vens.

Ou soit de Vienne et de Grenobles
Ly Dauphin, ly preux, ly senez,
Ou de Dijon, Salins et Doles,
Ly sires et ly filz ainsnez,
Ou autant de leurs gens privez,
Heraulx, trompetes, poursuivans,
Ont ilz bien bouté soubz le nez?
Autant en emporte ly vens.

Princes a mort sont destinez,
Et tous autres qui sont vivans;
S'ilz en sont courciez n'ataynez,
Autant en emporte ly vens.

SECOND BALLAD OF THE LORDS
OF OLD TIME

He keeps no more the holy See,
Albed and amiced as of old,
That pope of such strong sanctity
By his stole he'd grip and hold
Fiends ablaze, as I am told.
Rudely snuffed, this many a day,
With the least one of the fold,
And now upon the winds away.

Constantinople's majesty,
The emperor with fists of gold;
France's noblest monarch, he
Past earth's princes aureoled,
For great love to God. Behold,
What abbey stones he once would lay!
On every tongue their honour rolled,
And now upon the winds away.

No more their Dauphin's chivalry
Grenoble or Vienne unfold;
And in three towns of Burgundy
The lords with their firstborn are mould:
Knights and pursuivants untold,
Richly feasted in their day,
With trumpets and with heralds bold,
And now upon the winds away.

Death has princes in his fold;
Proud or subject, all our clay
Breathes a time, and then is cold,
And now upon the winds away.

Advis m'est que j'oy regreter
La belle qui fut hëaulmiere,
Soy jeune fille soushaitter
Et parler en telle maniere:
Ha! vieillesse felonne et fiere,
Pourquoi m'as si tost abatue?
Qui me tient, qui, que ne me fiere,
Et qu'a ce coup je ne me tue?

Tollu m'as la haulte franchise
Que beaulté m'avoit ordonné
Sur clers, marchans et gens d'Église:
Car lors il n'estoit homme né
Qui tout le sien ne m'eust donné,
Quoy qu'il en fust des repentailles,
Mais que luy eusse habandonné
Ce que reffusent truandailles.

A maint homme l'ay reffusé,
Qui n'estoit a moy grant sagesse,
Pour l'amour d'ung garson rusé,
Auquel j'en feiz grande largesse.
A qui que je feisse finesse,
Par m'ame, je l'amoye bien!
Or ne me faisoit que rudesse,
Et ne m'amoit que pour le mien.

Si ne me sceut tant détrayner,
Fouler aux piez, que ne l'aymasse,
Et m'eust il fait les rains trayner,
S'il m'eust dit que je le baisasse,
Que tous mes maulx je n'oubliasse.
Le glouton, de mal entechié,
M'embrassoit . . . J'en suis bien plus grasse!
Que m'en reste il? Honte et pechié.

THE REGRET OF THE FAIR ARMOURESS

The fancy has me I hear weep
That armouress, once so fair, and sigh
Her girlhood back, and that I keep
The very fashion of her cry:
As cruel thieving age, then why
So quick to pluck my time away?
And now, what stays me now, when I
Might die at my own hands today?

You, you stole those high emperies
That I in beauty's right took on
Over all men, of all degrees,
Merchant, clerk, and monkish one.
Yea, in the season that is done,
There was no mother's son was born
But gave all, shameless, and he won
What now the meanest creatures scorn.

Well have I scorned a score of men,
Such lover's folly in me rose
For a young rascal of them then.
If to the rest I have made shows
Of love for gain, to him, God knows,
I gave my charities untold,
Though all I got of him was blows,
And he cared only for my gold.

He could not use me half so ill
That I left loving him for this,
And might have trampled me at will.
When once he begged of me one kiss,
No wrong I bore could seem amiss.
A glutton boy, and foul with blame,
His kiss sufficed me then for bliss.
My profit now the sin; the shame.

Or est il mort, passé trente ans,
Et je remains vielle, chenue.
Quant je pense, lasse! au bon temps
Quelle fus, quelle devenue!
Quant me regarde toute nue,
Et je me voy si tres changiee,
Povre, seiche, megre, menue,
Je suis presque toute enragiee.

Qu'est devenu ce front poly,
Cheveulx blons, ces sourcils voultiz
Grant entroeil, ce regart joly,
Dont prenoie les plus soubtilz;
Ce beau nez droit grant ne petiz,
Ces petites joinctes oreilles,
Menton fourchu, cler vis traictiz,
Et ces belles levres vermeilles?

Ces gentes espaulles menues,
Ces bras longs et ces mains traictisses,
Petiz tetins, hanches charnues,
Eslevees, propres, faictisses
A tenir amoureuses lisses;
Ces larges rains, ce sadinet
Assis sur grosses fermes cuisses,
Dedens son petit jardinet?

Le front ridé, les cheveux gris,
Les sourcilz cheus, les yeulx estains,
Qui faisoient regars et ris
Dont mains marchans furent attains;
Nez courbes de beauté loingtains,
Oreilles pendantes, moussues,
Le vis pally, mort et destains,
Menton froncé, levres peaussues:

(48)

Dead, for these thirty years; and I
Am a grey woman and alone.
When I reflect what days are by,
What I was then, and what am grown;
Stare down this body of a crone,
Naked – the body that I had
Changed to this dried, pinched skin and bone,
I am almost like a thing mad.

Alas, what chances overtook
Bright locks, smooth temples, brows upspread,
And wide great eyes whose laughing look
Would turn a wizard's head!
The nose, the dimpling chin are sped;
The whole clear visage never dull,
Small, wrought ears in the shapely head,
And lips deep-red and beautiful.

Those polished shoulders which I wore,
The two arms, delicate and long,
The lovely hands, ah! mine no more.
The little breasts, the curving, strong
Round hips that to love's wars belong,
The broad loins where a jewel lay,
Between firm thighs, and in among
Its pleasant garden, where are they?

The temples seamed now, the hair grey;
The brow's line lost; and the eyes blear; –
Those eyes where mirth and glancing play
Was beckoning every comer near;
The nose bowed from its pride; the ear
Hairy and pendulous; the skin
Death-pale, discolored, mottled, sere;
And coarse, rough lips; and a peaked chin.

C'est d'umaine beaulté l'issue!
Les bras cours et les mains contraites,
Les espaulles toutes bossues;
Mamelles, quoy? toutes retraites;
Telles les hanches que les tetes;
Du sadinet, fy! Quant des cuisses
Cuisses ne sont plus, mais cuissetes
Grivelees comme saulcisses.

Ainsi le bon temps regretons
Entre nous, povres vielles sotes
Assises bas, a crouppetons,
Tout en ung tas comme pelotes,
A petit feu de chenevotes
Tost allumees, tost estaintes;
Et jadis fusmes si mignotes! . . .
Ainsi en prent a mains et maintes.

Our human beauty ends with these!
Shrunk arms, lean hands; and dispossessed
The shapely shoulders, framed to please,
By the crook-back and withered breast.
The paps slack, and the hips; the rest,
That jewel? Pah! The thighs so thin
They are two bags of bones at best,
And poor and specked as sausage-skin.

Thus wretched silly hags we weep
Our heyday here together; stray
In corners, huddled, like a heap
Of rag-ends bundled out of way;
Or crouching on our hunkers lay
Small fires of straw, soon caught, soon low –
The rare, the darlings of our day!
Time has robbed many others so.

BALLADE DE LA BELLE HEAULMIÈRE
AUX FILLES DE JOIE

Or y pensez, belle Gantiere
Qui m'escoliere souliez estre,
Et vous, Blanche la Savetiere,
Or est il temps de vous congnoistre.
Prenez a destre et a senestre;
N'espargnez homme, je vous prie:
Car vielles n'ont ne cours ne estre,
Ne que monnoye qu'on descrie.

Et vous, la gente Saulciciere
Qui de dancier estre adestre,
Guillemete la Tapiciere,
Ne mesprenez vers vostre maistre:
Tost vous fauldra clorre fenestre;
Quant deviendrez vielle, flestrie,
Plus ne servirez qu'ung viel prestre,
Ne que monnoye qu'on descrie.

Jehanneton la Chapperonniere,
Gardez qu'amy ne vous empestre;
Et Katherine la Bourciere,
N'envoyez plus les hommes paistre:
Car qui belle n'est, ne perpetre
Leur male grace, mais leur rie.
Laide viellesse amour n'empestre,
Ne que monnoye qu'on descrie.

Filles, vueillez vous entremettre
D'escouter pourquoy pleure et crie:
Pour ce que je ne me puis mettre,
Ne que monnoye qu'on descrie.

BALLAD AND CREED OF THE FAIR ARMOURESS
TO THE DAUGHTERS OF JOY

You lovely glover's mistress, who
Profess to have learnt much of me,
With Blanche, who loves or soles a shoe,
Come, learn what both your ends will be;
Then snatch, whatever hearts you see,
Right, left; for both shall be when old
Called in from beauty's currency:
We are coins which wear thin of gold.

And dainty sausage-seller, you,
While still your dancing heels are free,
And weaver's Guillemette, you too:
You are choice now, but nights shall be
Soon when you shut unwillingly
Your winking windows; faded, cold, –
Old priests might serve as well; for see
We are coins which wear thin of gold.

Jenny, to the hatter true,
May stop too long for such as he;
Spurmaster's Kate, when lovers sue,
Send no more packing so; ah me,
Let none show men discourtesy,
While her young favor may be sold.
Age is too ugly for love's fee,
We are coins which wear thin of gold.

Come all young wenches to my knee,
And learn I weep with cause, and scold,
But cannot turn from Time's decree:
We are coins which wear thin of gold.

Pour ce, amez tant que vouldrez,
Suyvez assemblees et festes,
En la fin ja mieulx n'en vauldrez
Et si n'y romprez que vos testes;
Folles amours font le gens bestes:
Salmon en ydolatria,
Samson en perdit ses lunetes.
Bien est eureux qui riens n'y a!

Orpheüs, le doux menestrier,
Jouant de fleustes et musetes,
En fut en dangier d'un murtrier
Chien Cerberus a quatre testes;
Et Narcisus, le bel honnestes,
En ung parfont puis s'en noya
Pour l'amour de ses amouretes.
Bien est eureux qui riens n'y a!

Sardana, le preux chevalier,
Qui conquist le regne de Cretes,
En voulut devenir moullier
Et filler entre pucelletes;
David le roy, sage prophetes,
Crainte de Dieu en oublia,
Voyant laver cuisses bien faites.
Bien est eureux qui riens n'y a!

Amon en voult deshonnourer,
Faignant de menger tarteletes,
Sa seur Thamar et desflourer,
Qui fut inceste deshonnestes;
Herodes, pas ne sont sornetes,
Saint Jehan Baptiste en decola
Pour dances, saulx et chansonnetes.
Bien est eureux qui riens n'y a!

DOUBLE BALLAD OF GOOD ADVICE

Who takes the wares love has for sale,
Such ills and pother of it buys,
It's well if heads be all that ail.
Poor silly loves so change the wise
They could great Solomon surprise
Praying to a painted show,
Samson blind in both his eyes.
Happier he who says No, no!

'Twas this snatched Orpheus from the vale,
Yes Orpheus, whose lute drew sighs,
Desire as low as hell could hale,
Where Cerberus' three dog-heads rise.
Alas, the chaste Narcissus' eyes
Saw in a pool some beauties show,
And now beneath the reeds he lies.
Happier he who says No, no!

Brave Sardona, a knight in mail,
Took Crete, and then in girl's disguise
Would after little maidens trail.
Was not the royal David wise?
He foretold death and paradise,
Yet even his fear of God would go
When a girl washed her pretty thighs.
Happier he who says No, no!

Or Ammon, coming with a tale
That just for little tarts he sighs,
On his own sister to prevail:
A sin of incest mixed with lies.
And more, and true as histories,
A leap brought Herod to bestow
John Baptist's head for a dancing prize!
Happier he who says No, no!

De moy, povre, je vueil parler:
J'en fus batu comme a ru telles,
Tout nu, ja ne le quier celer.
Qui me feist maschier ces groselles,
Fors Katherine de Vausselles?
Noel le tiers est, qui fut la.
Mitaines a ces nopces telles.
Bien est eureux qui riens n'y a!

Mais que ce jeune bacheler
Laissast ces jeunes bacheletes?
Non! et le deust on vif brusler
Comme ung chevaucheur d'escouvetes.
Plus doulces luy sont que civetes;
Mais toutesfoys fol s'y fya:
Soient blanches, soient brunetes,
Bien est eureux qui riens n'y a!

And I've a bruise or two to wail,
Flogged as when the washwench tries
To drub her dirty linen pale,
All naked, under Noel's eyes.
Who would so sour a shame devise?
Who but my lady, Katherine? O,
If love these blandishments applies,
Happier he who says No, no!

Yet turn a boy from loving? – Rail,
And swear you'll burn him if he sighs,
Stuck live above a blazing bale,
With hags who nightly whisk the skies,
A fool will always trust his eyes,
And girls as sweet as civet grow.
But blonde or brown, their sweets are lies.
Happier he who says No, no!

BALLADE QUE VILLON FEIST A LA REQUESTE
DE SA MÈRE POUR PRIER NOSTRE DAME

Dame du ciel, regente terrienne,
Emperiere des infernaux palus,
Recevez moy, vostre humble chrestienne,
Que comprinse soye entre vos esleus,
Ce non obstant qu'oncques rien ne valus.
Les biens de vous, ma Dame et ma Maistresse,
Sont trop plus grans que ne suis pecheresse,
Sans lesquelz biens ame ne peut merir
N'avoir les cieulx. Je n'en suis jangleresse:
En ceste foy je vueil vivre et mourir.

A vostre Filz dictes que je suis sienne;
De luy soyent mes pechiez abolus;
Pardonne moy comme a l'Egipcienne,
Ou comme il feist au clerc Theophilus,
Lequel par vous fut quitte et absolus,
Combien qu'il eust au deable fait promesse.
Preservez moy de faire jamais ce,
Vierge portant, sans rompure encourir,
Le sacrement qu'on celebre a la messe:
En ceste foy je vueil vivre et mourir.

Femme je suis povrette et ancïenne,
Qui riens ne sçay; oncques lettre ne lus.
Au moustier voy dont suis paroissienne
Paradis paint, ou sont harpes et lus,
Et ung enfer ou dampnez sont boullus:
L'ung me fait paour, l'autre joye et liesse.
La joye avoir me fay, haulte Deesse,
A qui pecheurs doivent tous recourir,
Comblez de foy, sans fainte ne paresse:
En ceste foy je vueil vivre et mourir.

HIS MOTHER'S SERVICE
TO OUR LADY

Lady of Heaven and earth, and therewithal
Crowned Empress of the nether clefts of Hell, –
I, thy poor Christian, on thy name do call,
Commending me to thee, with thee to dwell,
Albeit in nought I be commendable.
But all my undeserving may not mar
Such mercies as thy sovereign mercies are;
Without the which (as true words testify)
No soul can reach thy Heaven so fair and far.
Even in this faith I choose to live and die.

Unto thy Son say thou that I am His,
And to me graceless make Him gracious.
Sad Mary of Egypt lacked not of that bliss,
Nor yet the sorrowful clerk Theophilus,
Whose bitter sins were set aside even thus
Though to the Fiend his bounden service was.
Oh help me, lest in vain for me should pass
(Sweet Virgin that shalt have no loss thereby!)
The blessed Host and sacring of the Mass.
Even in this faith I choose to live and die.

A pitiful poor woman, shrunk and old,
I am, and nothing learn'd in letter-lore.
Within my parish-cloister I behold
A painted Heaven where harps and lutes adore,
And eke an Hell whose damned folk seethe full sore:
One bringeth fear, the other joy to me.
That joy, great Goddess, make thou mine to be, –
Thou of whom all must ask it even as I;
And that which faith desires, that let it see.
For in this faith I choose to live and die.

Vous portastes, digne Vierge, princesse,
Iesus regnant qui n'a ne fin ne cesse.
Le Tout Puissant, prenant nostre foiblesse,
Laissa les cieulx et nous vint secourir,
Offrit a mort sa tres chiere jeunesse;
Nostre Seigneur tel est, tel le confesse:
En ceste foy je vueil vivre et mourir.

O excellent Virgin Princess! thou didst bear
King Jesus, the most excellent comforter,
Who even of this our weakness craved a share
And for our sake stooped to us from on high,
Offering to death His young life sweet and fair.
Such as He is, our Lord, I Him declare,
And in this faith I choose to live and die.

BALLADE DES CONTRE VÉRITÉS

Il n'est soing que quant on a fain,
Ne service que d'ennemy,
Ne maschier qu'ung botel de foing,
Ne fort guet que d'homme endormy,
Ne clemence que felonnie,
N'asseurence que de peureux,
Ne foy que d'homme qui regnie,
Ne bien conseillé qu'amoureux.

Il n'est engendrement qu'en boing,
Ne bon bruit que d'homme banny,
Ne ris qu'après ung coup de poing,
Ne lotz que debtes mettre en ny,
Ne vraye amour qu'en flaterie,
N'encontre que de maleureux,
Ne vray rapport que menterie,
Ne bien conseillé qu'amoureux.

Ne tel repos que vivre en soing,
N'honneur porter que dire: «Fi!»,
Ne soy vanter que de faulx coing,
Ne santé que d'homme bouffy,
Ne hault vouloir que couardie,
Ne conseil que de furieux,
Ne doulceur qu'en femme estourdie,
Ne bien conseillé qu'amoureux.

Voulez vous que verté vous die?
Il n'est jouer qu'en maladie,
Lettre vraye que tragedie,
Lasche homme que chevalereux,
Orrible son que melodie,
Ne bien conseillé qu'amoureux.

BALLAD OF CONTRADICTIONS

Hungry folk are happiest,
Favors are of hatred bred,
Nourishment from straws is pressed,
Watch kept by the sleepyhead,
Clemency on felons shed.
Sinking hearts have confidence,
Broken vows were truly plead,
And only lovers have sound sense.

Exiles are reputed best,
Baths the likeliest bridal-bed;
Blows are parried with a jest,
Cheats alone are credited,
Long-face mopers banqueted;
Honest liking is pretence,
By rank falsehood truth is spread,
And only lovers have sound sense.

Carking care brings easy rest,
Fits and rages cool the head,
Reverence is by Fie! expressed;
Health is to be overfed,
Ventures are by poltroons led,
Wealth is counterfeited pence,
Shrews have gentlest speeches said,
And only lovers have sound sense.

By your leave I will attest
Gamesome are the sick-abed,
Laggard are the knightliest,
Downright talk has double sense,
Tune and dissonance are wed,
And only lovers have sound sense.

BALLADE DE VILLON A S'AMYE

Faulse beauté qui tant me couste chier,
Rude en effect, ypocrite doulceur,
Amour dure plus que fer a maschier,
Nommer que puis, de ma desfaçon seur,
Cherme felon, la mort d'ung povre cuer,
Orgueil mussié qui gens met au mourir,
Yeulx sans pitié, ne veult Droit de Rigueur,
Sans empirer, ung povre secourir?

Mieulx m'eust valu avoir esté serchier
Ailleurs secours: c'eust esté mon onneur;
Riens ne m'eust sceu lors de ce fait hachier.
Trotter m'en fault en fuyte et deshonneur.
Haro, haro, le grant et le mineur!
Et qu'esse cy? Mourray sans coup ferir?
Ou Pitié veult, selon ceste teneur,
Sans empirer, ung povre secourir?

Ung temps viendra qui fera dessechier,
Jaunir, flestrir vostre espanye fleur;
Je m'en risse, se tant peusse maschier
Lors; mais nennil, ce seroit donc foleur:
Viel je seray; vous, laide, sans couleur;
Or beuvez fort, tant que ru peut courir;
Ne donnez pas a tous ceste douleur,
Sans empirer, ung povre secourir.

Prince amoureux, des amans le greigneur,
Vostre mal gré ne vouldroye encourir,
Mais tout franc cuer doit pour Nostre Seigneur,
Sans empirer, ung povre secourir.

BALLAD TO HIS MISTRESS

Dishonored beauty, who have cost me so,
All harsh in works, so those sweet looks must be
Liars and false, your love a fiercer blow
Than thrusting steel: O charms attaint to me,
For killing of a heart, in felony,
Pride all contempt, and scorning that you kill,
Hard eyes, lies there in your inclemency
Some ease at last for woe, nor wound it still?

Would Heaven I had had the wit to go
When to have left her would have honored me,
Elsewhere for solace. None had wrung me so,
Then to this pitch. Now, flight, indignity,
Shunted, disgraced, with Haro, Charity!
Of great and little, O, of all that will;
And to die thus, save pity give, or she
Some ease at last for woe, nor wound it still.

When time shall droop your spreading petals low,
Perceiving them hang sick and yellowly,
If I own laughter then, I'll mock you so:
What mirth, alas, for madmen, would this be
That aged eyes should you all tintless see!
Go, long as streams shall run and drink your fill.
But never use the rest as you used me:
Some ease at last for woe, nor wound it still.

Great prince and lord of all love's mastery,
I am in nothing counter to thy will.
Christ knows true hearts will countersign this plea:
Some ease at last for woe, nor wound it still.

LAY

Mort, j'appelle de ta rigueur,
Qui m'as ma maistresse ravie,
Et n'es pas encore assouvie
Se tu ne me tiens en langueur:
Onc puis n'eus force ne vigueur;
Mais que te nuysoit elle en vie,
                Mort?

Deux estions et n'avions qu'ung cuer;
S'il est mort, force est que devie,
Voire, ou que je vive sans vie
Comme les images, par cuer,
                Mort!

TO DEATH, OF HIS LADY

Death, of thee do I make my moan,
Who hadst my lady away from me,
Nor wilt assuage thine enmity
Till with her life thou has mine own;
For since that hour my strength has flown.
Lo! what wrong was her life to thee,
       Death?

Two we were, and the heart was one;
Which now being dead, dead I must be,
Or seem alive as lifelessly
As in the choir the painted stone,
       Death!

BALLADE ET ORAISON

Pere Noé, qui plantastes la vigne,
Vous aussi, Loth, qui beustes ou rochier,
Par tel party qu'Amours, qui gens engigne,
De voz filles si vous feist approuchier
(Pas ne le dy pour le vous reprouchier),
Archetriclin, qui bien sceustes cest art,
Tous trois vous pry qu'o vous vueillez perchier
L'ame du bon feu maistre Jehan Cotart!

Jadis extraict il fut de vostre ligne,
Luy qui buvoit du meilleur et plus chier,
Et ne deust il avoir vaillant ung pigne;
Certes, sur tous, c'estoit ung bon archier;
On ne luy sceut pot des mains arrachier;
De bien boire ne fut oncques fetart.
Nobles seigneurs, ne souffrez empeschier
L'ame du bon feu maistre Jehan Cotart!

Comme homme beu qui chancelle et trepigne
L'ay veu souvent, quant il s'alloit couchier,
Et une fois il se feist une bigne,
Bien m'en souvient, a l'estal d'ung bouchier.
Brief, on n'eust sceu en ce monde serchier
Meilleur pyon, pour boire tost et tart.
Faictes entrer quant vous orrez huchier
L'ame du bon feu maistre Jehan Cotart!

Prince, il n'eust sceu jusqu'a terre crachier;
Tousjours crioit: «Haro! la gorge m'art.»
Et si ne sceust oncq sa seuf estanchier
L'ame du bon feu maistre Jehan Cotart.

BALLAD AND PRAYER FOR THE SOUL

Forefather Noah, who first set out the vine,
Lot, to the cave retired its fruits to try,
Till love, confusing sometimes, and the wine
Had brought you and your daughters pretty nigh,
(I bring this up though not to mortify)
Archetriclin, who bore a drinker's heart,
I pray all three of you deal fairly by
The soul of late lamented Jean Cotart.

Son and descendant of your ancient line,
He never had a penny to put by,
And always drank the best and dearest wine.
O, with a cask to shoot he could let fly,
And any jug that slipped his clutch was dry.
Present the bottle, he would do his part.
Sweet sirs, don't let them shut out from on high
The soul of late lamented Jean Cotart.

How often reel, trip, totter, intertwine
Used I his tipsy bedward feet espy!
That bang he got once of a butcher's sign,
I shall not soon forget. In short, lords, try
The whole world round you will not scare up, high
Or low, a worthier artist with a quart.
Open, when there mounts bellowing through the sky
The soul of late lamented Jean Cotart.

He could not spit far, Prince : it made him dry.
Help, Help, he screamed, My throat's a-fire. No art
Devised for quenching thirsts could satisfy
The soul of late lamented Jean Cotart.

BALLADE
POUR ROBERT D'ESTOUTEVILLE

Au poinct du jour, que l'esprevier s'esbat,
Meu de plaisir et par noble coustume,
Bruit la maulvis et de joye s'esbat,
Reçoit son per et se joinct a sa plume,
Offrir vous vueil, a ce desir m'alume,
Ioyeusement ce qu'aux amans bon semble.
Sachiez qu'Amour l'escript en son volume;
Et c'est la fin pour quoy sommes ensemble.

Dame serez de mon cuer sans debat,
Entierement, jusques mort me consume.
Lorier souef qui pour mon droit combat,
Olivier franc m'ostant toute amertume,
Raison ne veult que je desacoustume,
Et en ce vueil avec elle m'assemble,
De vous servir, mais que m'y acoustume;
Et c'est la fin pour quoy sommes ensemble.

Et qui plus est, quand dueil sur moy s'embat,
Par Fortune qui souvent si se fume,
Vostre doulx œil sa malice rabat,
Ne mais ne mains que le vent fait la plume.
Si ne pers pas la graine que je sume
En vostre champ, quant le fruit me ressemble.
Dieu m'ordonne que le fouÿsse et fume;
Et c'est la fin pour quoy sommes ensemble.

Princesse, oyez ce que cy vous resume:
Que le mien cuer du vostre desassemble
Ja ne sera; tant de vous en presume;
Et c'est la fin pour quoy sommes ensemble.

BALLAD WRITTEN FOR A BRIDEGROOM

Which Villon Gave to a Gentleman Newly Married to
Send to His Wife Whom He Had Won With the Sword

At daybreak, when the falcon claps his wings,
No whit for grief, but noble heart and high
With loud glad noise he stirs himself and springs,
And takes his meat, and toward his lure draws nigh;
Such good I wish you! Yea, and heartily
I am fired with hope of true love's meed to get;
Know that Love writes it in his book; for why,
This is the end for which we twain are met.

Mine own heart's lady with no gainsayings
You shall be always wholly till I die;
And in my right against all bitter things
Sweet laurel with fresh rose its force shall try;
Seeing reason wills not that I cast love by
(Not here with reason shall I chide or fret)
Nor cease to serve, but serve more constantly;
This is the end for which we twain are met.

And, which is more, when grief about me clings
Through Fortune's fit or fume of jealousy,
Your sweet kind eye beats down her threatenings
As wind doth smoke; such power sits in your eye.
Thus in your field my seed of harvestry
Thrives, for the fruit is like me that I set;
God bids me tend it with good husbandry;
This is the end for which we twain are met.

Princess, give ear to this my summary;
That heart of mine your heart's love should forget,
Shall never be: like trust in you put I:
This is the end for which we twain are met.

BALLADE

En realgar, en arcenic rochier,
En orpiment, en salpestre et chaulx vive,
En plomb boullant pour mieulx les esmorchier,
En suie et poix destrempez de lessive
Faicte d'estrons et de pissat de juifve,
En lavailles de jambes a meseaulx,
En racleure de piez et viels houseaulx,
En sang d'aspic et drogues venimeuses,
En fiel de loups, de regnars et blereaulx,
Soient frittes ces langues envieuses!

En cervelle de chat qui hayt peschier,
Noir, et si viel qu'il n'ait dent en gencive,
D'ung viel mastin, qui vault bien aussi chier,
Tout enragié, en sa bave et salive,
En l'escume d'une mulle poussive
Detrenchiee menu a bons ciseaulx,
En eaue ou ratz plongent groings et museaulx,
Raines, crappaulx et bestes dangereuses,
Serpens, lesars et telz nobles oyseaulx,
Soient frittes ces langues envieuses!

En sublimé, dangereux a touchier,
Et ou nombril d'une couleuvre vive,
En sang qu'on voit es palletes sechier
Sur ces barbiers, quant plaine lune arrive,
Dont l'ung est noir, l'autre plus vert que cive,
En chancre et fiz, et en ces ors cuveaulx
Ou nourrisses essangent leurs drappeaulx,
En petiz baings de filles amoureuses
(Qui ne m'entent n'a suivy les bordeaulx)
Soient frittes ces langues envieuses!

BALLAD OF SLANDEROUS TONGUES

With orpiment, with arsenic red and white
And boiling lead, for fitter fricassee
Quicklime, saltpetre, soot, and pitch unite
And in this mixture, tempered well with ley
Of Jewess' excrement, to think the bree;
In water that has lazars' legs made clean,
Wherein old boots and hosen steeped have been;
In aspics' blood, in deadly drugs and tried,
In badgers', wolves', and foxes' gall and spleen,
Let all these sharp and poisonous tongues be fried.

In brain of cat that water doth affright,
Black and so old that not a tooth has she;
In foam and slaver from a mad dog's bite,
Worthless for age, worn out and rickety;
In froth of broken-winded mule that ye
Have cut up small with shears; in water green
With festering slime, wherein there may be seen
Serpents and rats that there have lived and died,
Lizards, toads, frogs, and such like beasts obscene,
Let all these sharp and poisonous tongues be fried.

In sublimates, unsafe for mortal wight
To touch, that in a live snake's navel be;
In blood that, drying, when the moon's at height,
In barbers' bowls, now green as leeks, we see,
Now black, and in those tubs unsavourly,
Where soak the foul clouts of the midwife quean;
In bloody flux and cancerous pus venene;
In baths where whores themselves have purified,
(No apple-squire but knows the thing I mean,)
Let all these sharp and poisonous tongues be fried.

Prince, passez tous ces frians morceaulx,
S'estamine, sacs n'avez ou bluteaulx,
Parmy le fons d'unes brayes breneuses;
Mais, par avant, en estrons de pourceaulx
Soient frittes ces langues envieuses!

Prince, all these dainties look you strain and screen,
If sieve nor bag you have, nor yet tameen,
Through shitten hosen with the breech uptied;
But in swine's droppings, first, for greater teen,
Let all these sharp and poisonous tongues be fried.

Rencontré soit de bestes feu getans,
Que Jason vit, querant la toison d'or;
Ou transmué d'homme en beste sept ans,
Ainsi que fut Nabugodonosor;
Ou perte il ait et guerre aussi villaine
Que les Troyens pour la prinse d'Helaine;
Ou avallé soit avec Tantalus
Et Proserpine aux infernaulx palus;
Ou plus que Job soit en griefve souffrance,
Tenant prison en la tour Dedalus,
Qui mal vouldroit au royaulme de France!

Quatre mois soit en ung vivier chantans,
La teste au fons, ainsi que le butor;
Ou au Grant Turc vendu deniers contans,
Pour estre mis au harnois comme ung tor;
Ou trente ans soit, comme la Magdalaine,
Sans drap vestir de linge ne de laine;
Ou soit noyé comme fut Narcisus,
Ou aux cheveulx, comme Absalon, pendus
Ou, comme fut Judas, par Desperance;
Ou puist perir comme Simon Magus,
Qui mal vouldroit au royaulme de France!

D'Octovien puist revenir le tems:
C'est qu'on luy coule au ventre son tresor;
Ou qu'il soit mis entre meules flotans
En ung moulin, comme fut saint Victor;
Ou transglouty en la mer, sans aleine,
Pis que Jonas au corps de la baleine;
Ou soit banny de la clarté Phebus,
Des biens Juno et du soulas Venus,
Et du dieu Mars soit pugny a oultrance,
Ainsy que fut roy Sardanapalus,
Qui mal vouldroit au royaulme de France!

BALLAD AGAINST THE ENEMIES OF FRANCE

May he fall in with beasts that scatter fire,
Like Jason, when he sought the fleece of gold,
Or change from man to beast, three years entire,
As King Nebuchadnezzar did of old;
Or else have times as shameful and as bad
As Trojan folk for ravished Helen had;
Or gulfed with Proserpine and Tantalus
Let Hell's deep fen devour him dolorous,
With worse to bear than Job's worst sufferance,
Bound in his prison-maze with Dædalus,
Who could wish evil to the state of France!

May he four months, like bitterns in the mire,
Howl with head downmost in the lake-springs cold
Or to bear harness like strong bulls for hire
To the Great Turk for money down be sold;
Or thirty years like Magdalen live sad,
With neither wool nor web of linen clad;
Drown like Narciss', or swing down pendulous
Like Absalom with locks luxurious,
Or liker Judas fallen to reprobrance;
Or find such death as Simon sorcerous,
Who could wish evil to the state of France!

May the old times come of fierce Octavian's ire,
And in his belly molten coin be told;
May he like Victor in the mill expire,
Crushed between moving millstones on him rolled,
Or in deep sea drenched breathless, more adrad
Than in the whale's bulk Jonas, when God bade;
From Phoebus' light, from Juno's treasure-house
Driven, and from joys of Venus amorous,
And cursed of God most high to the utterance,
As was the Syrian king Antiochus,
Who could wish evil to the state of France!

Prince, porté soit des serfs Eolus
En la forest ou domine Glaucus;
Ou privé soit de paix et d'esperance:
Car digne n'est de posseder vertus
Qui mal vouldroit au royaulme de France!

Prince, may the bright-winged brood of Aeolus
To sea-king Glaucus' wild wood cavernous
Bear him bereft of peace and hope's least glance,
For worthless is he to get good of us,
Who could wish evil to the state of France!

BALLADE: LES CONTREDIZ DE FRANC GONTIER

Sur mol duvet assis, ung gras chanoine,
Lez ung brasier, en chambre bien natee,
A son costé gisant dame Sidoine,
Blanche, tendre, polie et attintee,
Boire ypocras, a jour et a nuytee,
Rire, jouer, mignonner et baisier,
Et nu a nu, pour mieulx des corps s'aisier,
Les vy tous deux, par ung trou de mortaise:
Lors je congneus que, pour dueil appaisier,
Il n'est tresor que de vivre a son aise:

Se Franc Gontier et sa compaigne Helaine
Eussent ceste doulce vie hantee,
D'oignons, civotz, qui causent forte alaine,
N'acontassent une bise tostee.
Tout leur mathon, ne toute leur potee,
Ne prise ung ail, je le dy sans noysier.
S'ilz se vantent couchier soubz le rosier,
Lequel vault mieulx? Lict costoyé de chaise?
Qu'en dites vous? Faut il a ce musier?
Il n'est tresor que de vivre a son aise.

De gros pain bis vivent, d'orge, d'avoine,
Et boivent eaue tout au long de l'anée.
Tous les oyseaulx d'icy en Babiloine
A tel escot une seule journee
Ne me tendroient, non une matinee.
Or s'esbate, de par Dieu, Franc Gontier,
Helaine o luy, soubz le bel esglantier:
Se bien leur est, cause n'ay qu'il me poise;
Mais, quoy que soit du laboureux mestier,
Il n'est tresor que de vivre a son aise.

Prince, jugiez, pour tous nous accorder.
Quant est de moy, mais qu'a nul ne desplaise,
Petit enfant, j'ay oÿ recorder:
Il n'est tresor que de vivre a son aise.

BALLAD DISPUTING FRANC-GONTIER

Once through a chink a merry priest I spied.
In a snug chamber and on down he lay,
His brazier bright, and Sidoine at his side,
The delicate white lady, tricked and gay.
Together would they laugh, toy, kiss and play,
Daylong, nightlong; drink Hippocras entwined,
Or lying naked easier pleasures find.
For through the mortar-chink I spied them there,
And since have sorrow's cure-all fast in mind;
Soft life a treasure is without compare.

O had Franc-Gontier and his Helen tried
So sweet a regimen, would they today
Heap onions up on crusts first hard, then dried,
Wake breathing leeks, and sup off curds and whey?
All sorrier stuff than garlic cloves, I say.
They boast their manners, I am not unkind.
They say they house in roses. To my mind
There's comfort in a right bed and a chair.
Need you or I consider much to find
Soft life a treasure is without compare.

They drink at springs, summer and winter tide,
With barley and with oats their bellies stay.
Not all the little singing birds which bide
From here to Babylon flute me away
A day or a forenoon to fare as they!
For God's sake leave Franc-Gontier reclined
Under the hawthorn bough, with all his kind.
I'm not oppressed that they are easy there;
But peasants' blisses will not move my mind.
Soft life a treasure is without compare.

The whole, Prince, to your judgment is consigned:
For my part, I would anger none, but swear
I have heard tell, and young was so inclined,
Soft life a treasure is without compare.

BALLADE DE LA GROSSE MARGOT

Se j'ayme et sers la belle de bon hait,
M'en devez vous tenir ne vil ne sot?
Elle a en soy des biens a fin souhait.
Pour son amour sains bouclier et passot;
Quant viennent gens, je cours et happe ung pot,
Au vin m'en fuis, sans demener grant bruit;
Je leur tens eaue, frommage, pain et fruit.
S'ilz paient bien, je leur dis: «Bene stat;
Retournez cy, quant vous serez en ruit,
En ce bordeau ou tenons nostre estat!»

Mais adoncques il y a grant deshait,
Quant sans argent s'en vient couchier Margot;
Veoir ne la puis, mon cuer a mort la hait.
Sa robe prens, demy saint et surcot,
Si luy jure qu'il tendra pour l'escot.
Par les costés se prent, «c'est Antecrist»
Crie, et jure par la mort Jhesucrist
Que non fera. Lors j'empoingne ung esclat;
Dessus son nez luy en fais ung escript,
En ce bordeau ou tenons nostre estat.

Puis paix se fait, et me fait ung gros pet,
Plus enfle qu'ung vlimeux escharbot.
Riant, m'assiet son poing sur mon sommet,
Gogo me dit, et me fiert le jambot.
Tous deux yvres, dormons comme ung sabot.
Et, au resveil, quant le ventre luy bruit,
Monte sur moy, que ne gaste son fruit.
Soubz elle geins, plus qu'un aiz me fait plat;
De paillarder tout elle me destruit,
En ce bordeau ou tenons nostre estat.

BALLAD OF VILLON AND MUCKLE MEG

Because I love and serve a whore sans glose,
Think not therefore or knave or fool am I:
She hath in her such goods as no man knows.
For love of her target and dirk I ply:
When clients come, I hend a pot therenigh
And get me gone for wine, without word said:
Before them water, fruit, bread, cheese, I spread.
If they pay well, I bid them "Well, God aid!
Come here again when you of lust are led,
In this the brothel where we ply our trade."

But surely before long an ill wind blows
When, coinless, Margot comes by me to lie.
I hate the sight of her, catch up her hose,
Her gown, her surcoat and her girdle-tie,
Swearing to pawn them, meat and drink to buy.
She grips me by the throat and cuffs my head,
Cries "Antichrist!" and swears by Jesus dead,
It shall not be: till I, to quell the jade,
A potsherd seize and I score her nose with red,
In this the brothel where we ply our trade.

Then she, peace made, to show we're no more foes,
A hugeous crack of wind at me lets fly
And laughing sets her fist against my nose,
Bids me "Go to" and claps me on the thigh;
Then, drunk, like logs we sleep, till, by and by,
Awaking, when her womb is hungerèd,
To spare the child beneath her girdlestead,
She mounts on me, flat as a pancake laid.
With wantoning she wears me to the thread,
In this the brothel where we ply our trade.

Vente, gresle, gelle, j'ay mon pain cuit.
Ie suis paillart, la paillarde me suit.
Lequel vault mieulx? Chascun bien s'entresuit.
L'ung vault l'autre; c'est a mau rat mau chat.
Ordure amons, ordure nous assuit;
Nous deffuyons onneur, il nous deffuit,
En ce bordeau ou tenons nostre estat.

Hail, rain, freeze, ready baked I hold my bread:
Well worth a lecher with a wanton wed!
Whether's the worse. They differ not a shred.
Ill cat to ill rat; each for each was made.
We flee from honour; it from us hath fled:
Lewdness we love, that stands us well in stead,
In this the brothel where we ply our trade.

BALLADE DES FEMMES DE PARIS

Quoy qu'on tient belles langagieres
Florentines, Veniciennes,
Assez pour estre messagieres,
Et mesmement les ancïennes;
Mais, soient Lombardes, Romaines,
Genevoises, a mes perilz,
Pimontoises, Savoisiennes,
Il n'est bon bec que de Paris.

De tres beau parler tiennent chaieres,
Ce dit on, les Neapolitaines,
Et sont tres bonnes caquetieres
Allemandes et Pruciennes;
Soient Grecques, Egipciennes,
De Hongrie ou d'autre pays,
Espaignolles ou Cathelennes,
Il n'est bon bec que de Paris.

Brettes, Suysses, n'y sçavent guieres,
Gasconnes, n'aussi Toulousaines:
De Petit Pont deux harengieres
Les concluront, et les Lorraines,
Engloises et Calaisiennes
(Ay je beaucoup de lieux compris?)
Picardes de Valenciennes;
Il n'est bon bec que de Paris.

Prince, aux dames Parisiennes
De beau parler donnez le pris;
Quoy qu'on die d'Italiennes,
Il n'est bon bec que de Paris.

BALLAD OF THE WOMEN OF PARIS

Such nimble chatterers they say,
And may say, Tuscan walls contain,
They spread the city news that way;
And Venice ladies, old, retain
Their speech. Go, search the Lombard plain,
Geneva, Rome, I stake my head,
Savoy and Piedmont, quite in vain,
The true magpies are Paris bred.

Women I hear by Naples bay
The summit of discourse attain.
In Prussia their tongues clack all day,
And all the next day clack again.
Against the nations I maintain,
And should if Catalonia plead,
Greece, Egypt, Hungary and Spain,
The true magpies are Paris bred.

Yes, female England and Calais,
Toulouse and Gascony might strain,
And prove mere lispers in the fray.
Why just two fishwives from the Seine
Could shut them up with all Lorraine,
With rivals from all quarters led,
The Picard, the Valencienne.
The true magpies are Paris bred.

O Prince our Paris ladies reign
As gossip's queens when all is said;
Italians may make matters plain,
The true magpies are Paris bred.

BALLADE
DU CONCOURS DE BLOIS

Je meurs de seuf auprès de la fontaine,
Chault comme feu, et tremble dent a dent;
En mon païs suis en terre loingtaine;
Lez ung brasier frissonne tout ardent;
Nu comme ung ver, vestu en president,
Je ris en pleurs et attens sans espoir;
Confort reprens en triste desespoir;
Je m'esjouïs et n'ay plaisir aucun;
Puissant je suis sans force et sans povoir,
Bien recueully, debouté de chascun.

Rien ne m'est seur que la chose incertaine;
Obscur, fors ce qui est tout evident;
Doubte ne fais, fors en chose certaine;
Science tiens a soudain accident,
Je gaigne tout et demeure perdent;
Au point du jour dis: «Dieu vous doint bon soir!»
Gisant envers, j'ay grant paour de cheoir;
J'ay bien de quoy et si n'en ay pas ung;
Eschoitte attens et d'omme ne suis hoir,
Bien recueully, debouté de chascun.

De rien n'ay soing, si mectz toute ma peine,
D'acquerir biens et n'y suis pretendent;
Qui mieulx me dit, c'est cil qui plus m'attaine,
Et qui plus vray, lors plus me va bourdent;
Mon amy est, qui me fait entendent
D'ung cigne blanc que c'est ung corbeau noir;
Et qui me nuyst, croy qu'il m'ayde a povoir;
Bourde, verté, au jour d'uy m'est tout un;
Je retiens tout, rien ne sçay concepvoir,
Bien recueully, debouté de chascun.

BALLAD WRITTEN BY VILLON UPON A SUBJECT PROPOSED BY CHARLES DUC D'ORLEANS

I die of thirst, although the spring's at hand;
Hot as a fire, my teeth with cold do shake:
In my own town, I'm in a foreign land;
Hard by a burning brazier do I quake;
Clad like a king, yet naked as a snake.
I laugh through tears, expect sans hope soe'er
And comfort take amiddleward despair;
Glad, though I joy in nought beneath the sun,
Potent am I, and yet as weak as air;
Well entertained, rebuffed of every one.

Nought's dim to me save what I understand;
Uncertain things alone for sure I take;
I doubt but facts that all unquestioned stand;
I'm only wise by chance for a whim's sake;
"Give you good-night!" I say, whenas I wake;
Lying at my length, of falling I beware;
I've goods enough, yet not a crown to spare!
Leave off a loser, though I still have won;
Await bequests although to none I'm heir;
Well entertained, rebuffed of every one.

I care for nought, yet all my life I've planned
Goods to acquire, although I've none at stake;
They speak me fairest, by whom most I'm banned,
And truest, who most mock of me do make:
He is my friend, who causes me mistake
Black ravens for white swans and foul for fair;
Who doth me hurt, I hold him debonair;
'Twixt truth and lying difference see I none;
Nought I conceive, yet all in mind I bear;
Well entertained, rebuffed of every one.

Prince clement, or vous plaise sçavoir
Que j'entens moult et n'ay sens ne sçavoir:
Parcial suis, a toutes loys commun.
Que fais je plus? Quoy? Les gaiges ravoir,
Bien recueully, debouté de chascun.

Most clement Prince, I'd have you be aware
That I'm like all, and yet apart and rare;
Much understand, yet wit and knowledge shun:
To have my wage again is all my care;
Well entertained, rebuffed of every one.

LA REQUESTE QUE VILLON BAILLA
A MONSEIGNEUR DE BOURBON

Le mien seigneur et prince redoubté,
Fleuron de lys, royalle geniture,
Françoys Villon, que Travail a dompté
A coups orbes, par force de bature,
Vous supplie par ceste humble escripture
Que lui faciez quelque gracieux prest.
De s'obliger en toutes cours est prest,
Si ne doubtez que bien ne vous contente:
Sans y avoir dommaige n'interest,
Vous n'y perdez seulement que l'attente.

A prince n'a ung denier emprunté,
Fors a vous seul, vostre humble creature.
De six escus que luy avez presté,
Cela pieça il meist en nourriture.
Tout se paiera ensemble, c'est droiture,
Mais ce sera legierement et prest;
Car, se du glan rencontre en la forest
D'entour Patay, et chastaignes ont vente,
Paié serez sans delay ny arrest:
Vous n'y perdrez seulement que l'attente.

Se je peusse vendre de ma santé
A ung Lombart, usurier par nature,
Faulte d'argent m'a si fort enchanté
Que j'en prendroie, ce cuide, l'adventure.
Argent ne pens a gippon n'a sainture;
Beau sire Dieux! je m'esbaïs que c'est
Que devant moy croix ne se comparoist,
Si non de bois ou pierre, que ne mente;
Mais s'une fois la vraye m'apparoist,
Vous n'y perdrez seulement que l'attente.

BALLAD OF VILLON'S REQUEST TO THE
DUC DE BOURBON

Gracious my lord and prince of mickle dread,
Flower of the Lily, Royal progeny,
François Villon, whom dule and teen have led
To the blind strokes of Fate to bend the knee,
Sues by this humble writing unto thee,
That thou wilt of thy grace to him make loan.
Before all courts his debit he will own:
Doubt not but he thy right will satisfy,
With interest thereunder due and grown:
Nothing but waiting shalt thou lose thereby.

Of no prince has thy creature borrowèd,
Save of thyself, a single penny fee:
The six poor crowns were wholly spent in bread,
That whiles thy favour did advance to me.
All shall be paid together, I agree,
And that right soon, ere many days be flown;
For if in Patay wood are acorns known
Or chestnuts thereabouts folk sell and buy
In season thou shalt have again thine own:
Nothing but waiting shalt thou lose thereby.

If I could sell my youth and lustihead
Unto the Lombards, usurers that be,
Lack-gold has brought me to such piteous stead,
I do believe I should the venture dree.
In purse or belt no money I can see:
I wonder what it is, by God His throne!
For unto me, save it be wood or stone,
No cross at all appears, – I do not lie:
But if the true cross once to me be shown,
Nothing but waiting shalt thou lose thereby.

Prince du lys, qui a tout bien complaist,
Que cuidez vous comment il me desplaist,
Quant je ne puis venir a mon entente?
Bien m'entendez; aidez moy, s'il vous plaist:
Vous n'y perdrez seulement que l'attente.

Prince of the Lys, that lov'st good deeds alone,
Think'st thou it has not cost me many a groan
That I cannot to my intent draw nigh?
Give ear, if it so please thee, to my moan:
Nothing but waiting shalt thou lose thereby.

BALLADE DES MENUS PROPOS

Je congnois bien mouches en let,
Je congnois a la robe l'homme,
Je congnois le beau temps du let,
Je congnois au pommier la pomme,
Je congnois l'arbre a veoir la gomme,
Je congnois quant tout est de mesmes,
Je congnois qui besongne ou chomme,
Je congnois tout, fors que moy mesmes.

Je congnois pourpoint au colet,
Je congnois le moyne a la gonne,
Je congnois le maistre au varlet.
Je congnois au voille la nonne,
Je congnois quant pipeur jargonne,
Je congnois fols nourris de cresmes,
Je congnois le vin a la tonne,
Je congnois tout, fors que moy mesmes.

Je congnois cheval et mulet,
Je congnois leur charge et leur somme,
Je congnois Bietris et Belet,
Je congnois get qui nombre et somme,
Je congnois vision et somme,
Je congnois la faulte des Boesmes,
Je congnois le povoir de Romme,
Je congnois tout, fors que moy mesmes.

Prince, je congnois tout en somme,
Je congnois coulourez et blesmes,
Je congnois Mort qui tout consomme,
Je congnois tout, fors que moy mesmes.

BALLAD OF THINGS KNOWN AND UNKNOWN

Flies in the milk I know full well:
I know men by the clothes they wear:
I know the walnut by the shell:
I know the foul sky from the fair:
I know the pear-tree by the pear:
I know the worker from the drone
And eke the good wheat from the tare:
I know all save myself alone.

I know the pourpoint by the fell
And by his gown I know the frère:
Master by varlet I can spell:
Nuns by the veils that hide their hair:
I know the sharper and his snare
And fools that fat on cates have grown:
Wines by the cask I can compare:
I know all save myself alone.

I know how horse from mule to tell:
I know the load that each can bear:
I know both Beatrice and Bell:
I know the hazards, odd and pair:
I know of visions in the air:
I know the power of Peter's throne
And how misled Bohemians were:
I know all save myself alone.

Prince, I know all things; fat and spare,
Ruddy and pale, to me are known:
And Death, that endeth all our care:
I know all save myself alone.

BALLADE DES PROVERBES

Tant grate chievre que mal gist,
Tant va le pot a l'eaue qu'il brise,
Tant chauffe on le fer qu'il rougist,
Tant le maille on qu'il se debrise,
Tant vault l'homme comme on le prise,
Tant s'eslongne il qu'il n'en souvient,
Tant mauvais est qu'on le desprise,
Tant crie l'on Noel qu'il vient.

Tant parle on qu'on se contredist,
Tant vault bon bruyt que grace acquise,
Tant promet on qu'on s'en desdist,
Tant prie on que chose est acquise,
Tant plus est chiere et plus est quise,
Tant la quiert on qu'on y parvient,
Tant plus commune et moins requise,
Tant crie l'on Noel qu'il vient.

Tant ayme on chien qu'on le nourrist,
Tant court chanson qu'elle est apprise,
Tant garde on fruit qu'il se pourrist,
Tant bat on place qu'elle est prise,
Tant tarde on que faut entreprise,
Tant se haste on que mal advient,
Tant embrasse on que chiet la prise,
Tant crie l'on Noel qu'il vient.

.   .   .

Prince, tant vit fol qu'il s'avise,
Tant va il qu'après il revient,
Tant le mate on qu'il se ravise,
Tant crie l'on Noel qu'il vient.

BALLAD OF PROVERBS

Goats scratch until they spoil their bed:
Pitcher to well too oft we send:
The iron's heated till it's red
And hammered till in twain it rend:
The tree grows as the twig we bend:
Men journey till they disappear
Even from the memory of a friend:
We shout out "Noel" till it's here.

Some mock until their hearts do bleed:
Some are so frank that they offend:
Some waste until they come to need:
A promised gift is ill to spend:
Some love God till from church they trend:
Wind shifts until to North it veer:
Till forced to borrow do we lend:
We shout out "Noel" till it's here.

Dogs fawn on us till them we feed:
Song's sung until by heart it's kenned:
Fruit's kept until it rot to seed:
The leaguered place falls in the end:
Folk linger till the occasion wend:
Haste oft throws all things out of gear:
One clips until the grasp's o'erstrained:
We shout out "Noel" till it's here.

Prince, fools live so long that they mend:
They go so far that they draw near:
They're cozened till they apprehend:
We shout out "Noel" till it's here.

BALLADE AU NOM DE LA FORTUNE

Fortune fus par clers jadis nommee,
Que toy, Françoys, crie et nomme murtriere,
Qui n'es homme d'aucune renommee.
Meilleur que toy fais user en plastriere,
Par povreté, et fouÿr en carriere;
S'a honte vis, te dois tu doncques plaindre?
Tu n'es pas seul; si ne te dois complaindre.
Regarde et voy de mes fais de jadis,
Mains vaillans homs par moy mors et roidis;
Et n'es, ce sçais, envers eulx ung souillon.
Appaise toy, et mets fin en tes dis.
Par mon conseil prens tout en gré, Villon!

Contre grans roys me suis bien anymee,
Le temps qui est passé ça en arriere:
Priam occis et toute son armee,
Ne luy valut tour, donjon, ne barriere;
Et Hannibal demoura il derriere?
En Cartaige par Mort le feis attaindre;
Et Scypion l'Affriquan feis estaindre;
Julles Cesar au Senat je vendis;
En Egipte Pompee je perdis;
En mer noyé Jason en ung bouillon;
Et une fois Romme et Rommains ardis.
Par mon conseil prens tout en gré, Villon!

Alixandre, qui tant feist de hemee,
Qui voulut veoir l'estoille pouciniere,
Sa personne par moy fut envlimee;
Alphasar roy, en champ, sur sa baniere
Rué jus mort. Cela est ma maniere,
Ainsi l'ay fait, ainsi le maintendray:

BALLAD OF FORTUNE

I of old time by makers Fortune hight –
Whom, François, thou dost rail at and decry, –
Far better men than thou, poor nameless wight,
I grind into the dust with poverty
And gar them delve i' the quarries till they die:
Wherefore complainest thou? If thou live ill,
Thou art not singular: so, peace, be still.
Think but how many mighty men of yore
I've laid stark dead to stiffen in their gore,
By whom thou'rt but a scullion knave perdie.
Content thee, then, and chide thy fate no more;
I rede thee, Villon, take it all in gree.

Oft have I girded me to wreak my spite
Upon great kings: lo, in the days gone by,
Priam I slew; and all his warlike might
Availed him nought, towers, walls nor ramparts high.
'Gainst Hannibal no less did I apply,
Who was attaint in Carthage by my skill:
And Scipio Africanus did I kill:
Great Caesar to the Senate I gave o'er
And wrecked stout Pompey upon Egypt shore:
Jason I drowned by tempest on the sea
And burned both Rome and Romans heretofore:
I rede thee, Villon, take it all in gree.

Nay, Alexander, that renownèd knight,
Who longed to reach the backward of the sky
And shed much blood, with poison did I blight;
I made Arphaxad on the field to lie,
Dead, by his royal standard. Thus did I
Full many a time and yet more will fulfil:

Autre cause ne raison n'en rendray.
Holofernes l'ydolastre mauldis,
Qu'occist Judith (et dormoit entandis!)
De son poignart, dedens son pavillon;
Absalon, quoy? en fuyant le pendis.
Par mon conseil prens tout en gré, Villon!

Pour ce, Françoys, escoute que te dis:
Se riens peusse sans Dieu de Paradis,
A toy n'autre ne demourroit haillon,
Car, pour ung mal, lors j'en feroye dix.
Par mon conseil prens tout en gré, Villon!

Nor time nor reason can awry my will.
Huge Holophernes, too, that did adore
Strange gods, whom Judith with his sword of war
Slew as he slept; and Absalom, as he
Fled, by the lovelocks hanged I that he wore.
I rede thee, Villon, take it all in gree.

Poor François, set my rede in thy heart's core:
If I could aught without God's leave or lore,
I'd leave no rag to one of all that be;
For each ill done I'd compass half a score:
I rede thee, Villon, take it all in gree.

RONDEAU

Jenin l'Avenu,
Va-t-en aux estuves;
Et toy la venu,
Jenin l'Avenu,

Si te lave nud
Et te baigne es cuves.
Jenin l'Avenu,
Va-t-en aux estuves.

JENIN L'AVENU

Jenin l'Avenu,
Quick, while the baths are hot,
Go, get a scrub, shoo!
Jenin l'Avenu.

Strip yourself first, too,
Wash in the boiler-pot,
Jenin l'Avenu,
Quick, while the baths are hot.

Beaulx enfans, vous perdez la plus
Belle rose de vo chappeau;
Mes clers pres prenans comme glus,
Se vous allez a Montpipeau
Ou a Rueil, gardez la peau:
Car, pour s'esbattre en ces deux lieux,
Cuidant que vaulsist le rappeau,
Le perdit Colin de Cayeux.

Ce n'est pas ung jeu de trois mailles,
Ou va corps, et peut estre l'ame.
Qui pert, riens n'y sont repentailles
Qu'on n'en meure a honte et diffame;
Et qui gaigne n'a pas a femme
Dido la royne de Cartage.
L'homme est donc bien fol et infame
Qui, pour si peu, couche tel gage.

Qu'ung chascun encore m'escoute!
On dit, et il est vérité,
Que charterie se boit toute,
Au feu l'yver, au bois l'esté:
S'argent avez, il n'est ènté,
Mais le despèndez tost et viste.
Qui en voyez vous herité?
Jamais mal acquest ne prouffite.

PRETTY LESSON FOR STRAY BOYS

Ah, jaunty striplings, you let fall
That rose best trims your caps at last!
Though learned like birdlime to snare all,
My scholars, till Montpipeau's passed,
And Rueil, see your skins are fast.
Once playing there, and trusting so
The worth of an appeal was vast,
Colin de Cayeux let his go.

You toss no pennies now, but lay
Both souls and lives as this throw fall;
For he who loses at the play
Dies shamed, though he repent it all.
Nor can the luckiest of you call
Even Queen Dido his thereby.
Harebrained and wretches, if you shall
For your mean winnings risk so high.

And more, there is a saying runs,
And Truth's own lips have shaped it so:
A tavern's wines, in brimmed-up tuns,
Are soon by winter fires drunk low,
Or under summer boughs. Ah no,
Sin had not ever much to share.
Gold you may get, and gold will go,
Nor leave its spendthrift as its heir.

BALLADE DE BON CONSEIL

Hommes faillis, bersaudez de raison,
Desnaturez et hors de congnoissance,
Desmis du sens, comblez de desraison,
Fols abusez, plains de descongnoissance,
Qui procurez contre vostre naissance,
Vous soubzmettans a detestable mort
Par lascheté las! que ne vous remort
L'orribleté qui a honte vous maine?
Voyez comment maint jeunes homs est mort
Par offenser et prendre autruy demaine.

Chascun en soy voye sa mesprison,
Ne nous venjons, prenons en pacience;
Nous congnoissons que ce monde est prison
Aux vertueux franchis d'impatience;
Battre, rouiller, pour ce n'est pas science,
Tollir, ravir, piller, meurtrir a tort.
De Dieu ne chault, trop de verté se tort
Qui en telz faiz sa jeunesse demaine,
Dont a la fin ses poins doloreux tort
Par offenser et prendre autruy demaine.

Que vault piper, flater, rire en trayson,
Quester, mentir, affermer sans fiance,
Farcer, tromper, artifier poison,
Vivre en perchié, dormir en deffiance
De son prouchain sans avoir confiance?
Pour ce conclus: de bien faisons effort,
Reprenons cuer, ayons en Dieu confort,
Nous n'avons jour certain en la sepmaine;
De nos maulx ont noz parens le ressort
Par offenser et prendre autruy demaine.

BALLAD OF GOOD COUNSEL

O men, what lost and blinded course you run,
So reasonless, so base we no more know
If you be men; what folly's wreath have won!
Fools, and abusing even folly so,
Turning against your very throats the blow
Of death, and death by shame; so little brave
You yield that space of life which fortune gave,
Have you no dread at heart, no pricking sorrow,
Seeing how many a boy has found the grave,
Who filched or robbed another of his morrow?

We have been sorely spited every one,
And given cramping quarters here below,
But vent no grudges for what fate has done.
The virtuous have not chafed as you, but know
If not much is allotted, less even so
Thieves, ruffians, cut-throats, rogues and ravishers save.
It is not God who errs, but you who brave
Your time of youth out so to end in sorrow.
They twist at length two anguished fists and rave,
Who filched or robbed another of his morrow.

Use all your smiles for fools-bait. What is won?
Deal treacheries, lies, snares, poisons out; and go
On shifty credit: all for what? To run
Rascal by day, and in your chamber know
You sleep with your next neighbor as your foe.
Mend then, as you best can, and mending have
Both heart again, and solace. God will save.
No day of life is ours except to borrow.
Kindred are shamed, left mourning for a knave
Who filched or robbed another of his morrow.

Vivons en paix, exterminons discort;
Ieunes et vieulx, soyons tous d'ung accort:
La loy le veult, l'apostre le ramaine
Licitement en l'epistre rommaine;
Ordre nous fault, estat ou aucun port.
Notons ces poins; ne laissons le vray port
Par offenser et prendre autruy demaine.

Live we, both young and old, as law would have,
By those instructions the apostle gave;
He bade the Romans be at peace. Then borrow
His word to them. Of discord comes all sorrow.
Salvation, order, surety we crave.
Seek these, nor do as misled wretches have
Who filched or robbed another of his morrow.

BALLADE DE BONNE DOCTRINE A CEUX DE MAUVAISE VIE

Car ou soies porteur de bulles,
Pipeur ou hasardeur de dez,
Tailleur de faulx coings et te brusles
Comme ceulx qui sont eschaudez,
Traistres parjurs, de foy vuidez;
Soies larron, ravis ou pilles:
Ou en va l'acquest, que cuidez?
Tout aux tavernes et aux filles.

Ryme, raille, cymballe, luttes,
Comme fol, fainctif, eshontez;
Farce, broulle, joue des fleustes;
Fais, es villes et es citez,
Farces, jeux et moralitez;
Gaigne au berlanc, au glic, aux quilles:
Aussi bien va, or escoutez!
Tout aux tavernes et aux filles.

De telz ordures te reculles,
Laboure, fauche champs et prez,
Sers et pense chevaux et mulles,
S'aucunement tu n'es lettrez;
Assez auras, se prens en grez.
Mais, se chanvre broyes ou tilles,
Ne tens ton labour qu'as ouvrez
Tout aux tavernes et aux filles?

Chausses, pourpoins esguilletez,
Robes, et toutes vos drappilles,
Ains que vous fassiez pis, portez
Tout aux tavernes et aux filles.

VILLON'S STRAIGHT TIP
TO ALL CROSS COVES

Suppose you screeve? or go cheap-jack?
Or fake the broads? or fig a nag?
Or thimble-rig? or knap a yack?
Or pitch a snide? or smash a rag?
Suppose you duff? or nose and lag?
Or get the straight, and land your pot?
How do you melt the multy swag?
Booze and the blowens cop the lot.

Fiddle or fence, or mace, or mack,
Or moskeneer, or flash the drag;
Dead-lurk a crib, or do a crack,
Pad with a slang, or chuck a fag;
Bonnet, or tout, or mump and gag;
Rattle the tats, or mark the spot:
You cannot bag a single stag –
Booze and the blowens cop the lot.

Suppose you try a different tack,
And on the square you flash your flag?
At penny-a-lining make your whack,
Or with the mummers mump and gag?
For nix, for nix, the dibs you bag!
At any graft, no matter what,
Your merry goblins soon stravag, –
Booze and the blowens cop the lot.

It's up the spout and Charley Wag
With wipes and tickers and what not;
Until the squeezer nips your scrag,
Booze and the blowens cop the lot.*

* For a more understandable if less colorful version, see the Appendix.

ÉPISTRE EN FORME DE BALLADE
A SES AMIS

Aiez pitié, aiez pitié de moy,
A tout le moins, si vous plaist, mes amis!
En fosse gis, non pas soubz houx ne may,
En cest exil ouquel je suis transmis
Par Fortune, comme Dieu l'a permis.
Filles amans jeunes gens et nouveaulx,
Danceurs, saulteurs, faisans les piez de veaux,
Vifz comme dars, agus comme aguillon,
Gousiers tintans cler comme cascaveaux,
Le lesserez la, le povre Villon?

Chantres chantans a plaisance, sans loy,
Galans, rians, plaisans en fais et dis,
Courens alans, francs de faulx or, d'aloy,
Gens d'esperit, ung petit estourdis,
Trop demourez, car il meurt entandis.
Faiseurs de laiz, de motetz et rondeaux,
Quant mort sera, vous lui ferez chaudeaux!
Ou gist, il n'entre escler ne tourbillon:
De murs espoix on lui a fait bandeaux.
Le lesserez la, le povre Villon?

Venez le veoir en ce piteux arroy,
Nobles hommes, francs de quart et de dix,
Qui ne tenez d'empereur ne de roy,
Mais seulement de Dieu de Paradis:
Jeuner lui fault dimenches et merdis,
Dont les dens a plus longues que ratteaux;
Après pain sec, non pas après gasteaux,
En ses boyaulx verse eaue a gros bouillon;
Bas en terre, table n'a ne tresteaulx.
Le lesserez la, le povre Villon?

EPISTLE IN FORM OF A BALLAD
TO HIS FRIENDS

Have pity, pity, friends, have pity on me,
Thus much, at least, may it please you, of your grace!
I lie not under hazel or hawthorn-tree
Down in this dungeon ditch, mine exile's place
By leave of God and fortune's foul disgrace.
Girls, lovers, glad young folk and newly wed,
Jumpers and jugglers, tumbling heel o'er head,
Swift as a dart, and sharp as needle-ware,
Throats clear as bells that ring the kine to shed,
Your poor old friend, what, will you leave him there?

Singers that sing at pleasure, lawlessly,
Light, laughing, gay of word and deed, that race
And run like folk light-witted as ye be
And have in hand nor current coin nor base,
Ye wait too long, for now he's dying apace.
Rhymers of lays and roundels sung and read,
Ye'll brew him broth too late when he lies dead.
Nor wind nor lightning, sunbeam nor fresh air,
May pierce the thick wall's bound where lies his bed;
Your poor old friend, what, will you leave him there?

O noble folk from tithes and taxes free,
Come and behold him in this piteous case,
Ye that nor king nor emperor holds in fee,
But only God in heaven; behold his face
Who needs must fast, Sundays and holidays,
Which makes his teeth like rakes; and when he hath fed
With never a cake for banquet but dry bread,
Must drench his bowels with much cold watery fare,
With board nor stool, but low on earth instead;
Your poor old friend, what, will you leave him there?

Princes nommez, ancïens, jouvenceaux,
Impetrez moy graces et royaulx seaux,
Et me montez en quelque corbillon.
Ainsi le font, l'un a l'autre, pourceaux,
Car, ou l'un brait, ilz fuyent a monceaux.
Le lesserez la, le povre Villon?

Princes afore-named, old and young foresaid,
Get me the king's seal and my pardon sped,
And hoist me in some basket up with care:
So swine will help each other ill bested,
For where one squeaks they run in heaps ahead.
Your poor old friend, what, will you leave him there?

L'ÉPITAPHE EN FORME DE BALLADE

Que feit Villon pour lui et ses compagnons,
s'attendant estre pendu avec eux

Freres humains qui après nous vivez,
N'ayez les cuers contre nous endurcis,
Car, se pitié de nous povres avez,
Dieu en aura plus tost de vous mercis.
Vous nous voiez cy attachez cinq, six:
Quant de la chair, que trop avons nourrie,
Elle est pieça devorée et pourrie,
Et nous, les os, devenons cendre et pouldre.
De nostre mal personne ne s'en rie;
Mais priez Dieu que tous nous vueille absouldre!

Se freres vous clamons, pas n'en devez
Avoir desdaing, quoy que fusmes occis
Par justice. Toutesfois, vous sçavez
Que tous hommes n'ont pas bon sens rassis;
Excusez nous, puis que sommes transsis,
Envers le fils de la Vierge Marie,
Que sa grace ne soit pour nous tarie,
Nous preservant de l'infernale fouldre.
Nous sommes mors, ame ne nous harie;
Mais priez Dieu que tous nous vueille absouldre!

La pluye nous a debuez et lavez,
Et le soleil dessechiez et noircis;
Pies, corbeaulx, nous ont les yeux cavez,
Et arrachié la barbe et les sourcis.
Jamais nul temps nous ne sommes assis;
Puis çà, puis la, comme le vent varie,
A son plaisir sans cesser nous charie,
Plus becquetez d'oiseaulx que dez a couldre.
Ne soiez donc de nostre confrairie;
Mais priez Dieu que tous nous vueille absouldre!

THE EPITAPH IN FORM OF A BALLAD

Which Villon Made for Himself and His Comrades,
   Expecting to Be Hanged Along with Them

Men, brother men, that after us yet live,
Let not your hearts too hard against us be;
For if some pity of us poor men ye give,
The sooner God shall take of you pity.
Here are we five or six strung up, you see,
And here the flesh that all too well we fed
Bit by bit eaten and rotten, rent and shred,
And we the bones grow dust and ash withal;
Let no man laugh at us discomforted,
But pray to God that he forgive us all.

If we call on you, brothers, to forgive,
Ye should not hold our prayer in scorn, though we
Were slain by law; ye know that all alive
Have not wit alway to walk righteously;
Make therefore intercession heartily
With him that of a virgin's womb was bred,
That his grace be not as a dry well-head
For us, nor let hell's thunder on us fall;
We are dead, let no man harry or vex us dead,
But pray to God that he forgive us all.

The rain has washed and laundered us all five,
And the sun dried and blackened; yea, perdie,
Ravens and pies with beaks that rend and rive
Have dug our eyes out and plucked off for fee
Our beards and eyebrows; never are we free,
Not once, to rest; but here and there still sped,
Drive at its wild will by the wind's change led,
More pecked of birds than fruits on garden-wall;
Men, for God's love, let no gibe here be said,
But pray to God that he forgive us all.

Prince Jhesus, qui sur tous a maistre,
Garde qu'Enfer n'ait de nous seigneurie:
A luy n'ayons que faire ne que souldre.
Hommes, icy n'a point de mocquerie;
Mais priez Dieu que tous nous vueille absouldre!

Prince Jesus, that of all art lord and head,
Keep us, that hell be not our bitter bed;
We have nought to do in such a master's hall.
Be not ye therefore of our fellowhead,
But pray to God that he forgive us all.

LE QUATRAIN QUE FEIT VILLON
QUAND IL FUT JUGÉ A MOURIR

Je suis Françoys, dont il me poise,
Né de Paris emprès Pontoise,
Et de la corde d'une toise
Sçaura mon col que mon cul poise.

THE QUATRAIN THAT VILLON MADE
WHEN HE WAS DOOMED TO DIE

François am I, – woe worth it me!
At Paris born, near Pontoise citie,
Whose neck, in the bight of a rope of three,
Must prove how heavy my buttocks be.

VARIANT OF THE FOREGOING EPITAPH

François am I, – woe worth it me!
– Corbier my surname is aright:
Native of Auvers, near Pontoise citie;
Of folk for sobriquet Villon hight.
But for the gallant appeal I made,
My neck in the bight of a rope of three,
Had known ere this what my buttocks weighed.
The game scarce seemed to me worth to be played.

LE DÉBAT DU CUER ET DU CORPS
DE FRANÇOIS VILLON

Qu'est ce que j'oy? – Ce suis je! – Qui? – Ton cuer,
Qui ne tient mais qu'a ung petit filet:
Force n'ay plus, substance ne liqueur,
Quant je te voy retraict ainsi seulet,
Com povre chien tapy en reculet. –
Pour quoy est ce? – Pour ta folle plaisance. –
Que t'en chault il? – J'en ay la desplaisance. –
Laisse m'en paix! – Pour quoy? – J'y penserai. –
Quant sera ce? – Quant seray hors d'enfance. –
Plus ne t'en dis. – Et je m'en passeray. –

Que penses tu? – Estre homme de valeur. –
Tu as trente ans: c'est l'aage d'un mullet;
Est ce enfance? – Nennil. – C'est donc folleur
Qui te saisist? – Par ou? Par le collet? –
Rien ne congnois. – Si fais. – Quoy? – Mouche en let;
L'ung est blanc, l'autre est noir, c'est la distance. –
Est ce donc tout? – Que veulx tu que je tance?
Se n'est assez, je recommenceray. –
Tu es perdu! – J'y mettray resistance. –
Plus ne t'en dis. – Et je m'en passeray. –

J'en ay le dueil; toy, le mal et douleur.
Se feusses ung povre ydiot et folet,
Encore eusses de t'excuser couleur:
Si n'as tu soing, tout t'est ung, bel ou let.
Ou la teste as plus dure qu'ung jalet,
Ou mieulx te plaist qu'onneur ceste meschance!
Que respondras a ceste consequence? –
J'en seray hors quant je trespasseray. –
Dieu, quel confort! – Quelle sage eloquence! –
Plus ne t'en dis. – Et je m'en passeray. –

THE DISPUTE OF THE HEART AND BODY
OF FRANÇOIS VILLON

Who is this I hear? – Lo, this is I, thine heart,
That holds on merely now by a slender string.
Strength fails me, shape and sense are rent apart,
The blood in me is turned to a bitter thing,
Seeing thee skulk here like a dog shivering. –
Yea, and for what? – For that thy sense found sweet. –
What irks it thee? – I feel the sting of it. –
Leave me at peace. – Why? – Nay now, leave me at peace;
I will repent when I grow ripe in wit. –
I say no more. – I care not though thou cease. –

What art thou, trow? – A man worth praise perfay. –
This is thy thirtieth year of wayfaring. –
'Tis a mule's age. – Art thou a boy still? – Nay. –
Is it hot lust that spurs thee with its sting,
Grasping thy throat? Know'st thou not anything? –
Yea, black and white, when milk is speckled with flies,
I can make out. – No more? – Nay, in no wise.
Shall I begin again the count of these? –
Thou art undone. – I will make shift to rise. –
I say no more. – I care not though thou cease. –

I have the sorrow of it, and thou the smart.
Wert thou a poor mad fool or weak of wit,
Then might'st thou plead this pretext with thine heart;
But if thou know not good from evil a whit
Either thy head is hard as stone to hit,
Or shame, not honour, gives thee most content.
What canst thou answer to this argument? –
When I am dead I shall be well at ease. –
God! What good luck. – Thou art over eloquent. –
I say no more. – I care not though thou cease. –

Dont vient ce mal? – Il vient de mon maleur.
Quant Saturne me feist mon fardelet,
Ces maulx y meist, je le croy. – C'est foleur:
Son seigneur es, et te tiens son varlet.
Voy que Salmon escript en son rolet:
«Homme sage, ce dit il, a puissance
Sur planetes et sur leur influence.» –
Je n'en croy riens; tel qu'ilz m'ont fait seray. –
Que dis tu? – Dea! certes, c'est ma creance. –
Plus ne t'en dis. – Et je m'en passeray.

Veulx tu vivre? – Dieu m'en doint la puissance! –
Il te fault . . . – Quoy? – Remors de conscience,
Lire sans fin. – En quoy? – Lire en science,
Laisser les folz! – Bien j'y adviseray. –
Or le retien! – J'en ay bien souvenance. –
N'atens pas tant que tourne a desplaisance.
Plus ne t'en dis. – Et je m'en passeray.

Whence is this ill? – From sorrow and not from sin.
When Saturn packed my wallet up for me
I well believe he put these ills therein. –
Fool, wilt thou make thy servant lord of thee?
Hear now the wise king's counsel; thus saith he:
All power upon the stars a wise man hath;
There is no planet that shall do him scathe. –
Nay, as they made me I grow and I decrease. –
What say'st thou? – Truly, this is all my faith. –
I say no more. – I care not though thou cease. –

Would'st thou live still? – God help me that I may! –
Then thou must – What? Turn penitent and pray? –
Read always – What? – Grave words and good to say;
Leave off the ways of fools lest they displease. –
Good; I will do it. – Wilt thou remember? – Yea. –
Abide not till there come an evil day.
I say no more. – I care not though thou cease.

LA REQUESTE DE VILLON PRESENTÉE
A LA COUR DE PARLEMENT
EN FORME DE BALLADE

Tous mes cinq sens: yeulx, oreilles et bouche,
Le nez, et vous, le sensitif aussi;
Tous mes membres ou il y a reprouche,
En son endroit ung chascun die ainsi:
‹‹Souvraine Court, par qui sommes icy,
Vous nous avez gardé de desconfire.
Or la langue seule ne peut souffire
A vous rendre souffisantes louenges;
Si parlons tous, fille du souvrain Sire,
Mere des bons et seur des benois anges!››

Cuer, fendez vous, ou percez d'une broche,
Et ne soyez, au moins, plus endurcy
Qu'au desert fut la forte bise roche
Dont le peuple des Juifs fut adoulcy:
Fondez lermes et venez a mercy;
Comme humble cuer qui tendrement souspire,
Louez la Court, conjointe au Saint Empire,
L'eur des Françoys, le confort des estranges,
Procreee lassus ou ciel empire,
Mere des bons et seur des benois anges!

Et vous, mes dens, chascune si s'esloche;
Saillez avant, rendez toutes mercy,
Plus hautement qu'orgue, trompe, ne cloche
Et de maschier n'ayez ores soussy;
Considerez que je feusse transsy,
Foye, pommon et rate, qui respire;
Et vous, mon corps, qui vil estes et pire
Qu'ours, ne pourceau qui fait son nyt es fanges,
Louez la Court, avant qu'il vous empire,
Mere des bons et seur des benois anges!

THE REQUEST OF VILLON PRESENTED TO THE
HIGH COURT OF PARLIAMENT
IN BALLAD FORM

All my five senses, in your several place,
Hearing and seeing, taste and touch and smell,
Every my member branded with disgrace, –
Each on this fashion do ye speak and tell:
"Most Sovereign Court, by whom we here befell,
Thou that deliveredst us from sore dismays,
The tongue sufficeth not thy name to blaze
Forth in such strain of honor as it should:
Wherefore to thee our voices all we raise,
Sister of angels, mother of the good!"

Heart, cleave in sunder, or in any case
Be not more hardened and impermeable
Than was the black rock in the desert-space,
Which with sweet water for the Jews did swell;
Melt into tears and mercy call, as well
Befits a lowly heart that humbly prays:
Give to the Court, the kingdom's glory, praise, –
The Frenchman's stay, the help of strangerhood,
Born of high heaven amidst the empyreal rays:
Sister of angels, mother of the good!

And you, my teeth, your sockets leave apace;
Come forward, all, and loudlier than bell,
Organ or clarion, render thanks for grace
And every thought of chewing now repel.
Bethink you, I was doomed to death and hell,
Heart, spleen and liver palsied with affrays:
And you, my body, (else you were more base
Than bear or swine that in the dunghill brood),
Extol the Court, ere worser hap amaze;
Sister of angels, mother of the good!

Prince, trois jours ne vueillez m'escondire,
Pour moy pourveoir et aux miens ‹‹a Dieu›› dire;
Sans eulx argent je n'ay, icy n'aux changes.
Court triumphant, fiat, *sans me desdire,*
Mere des bons et seur des benois anges!

Prince, of thy grace, deny me not three days
To bid my friends adieu and go my ways:
Without them I've nor money, clothes nor food.
Triumphant Court, be't as thy suppliant says;
Sister of angels, mother of the good!

Que vous semble de mon appel,
Garnier? Feis je sens ou folie?
Toute beste garde sa pel;
Qui la contraint, efforce ou lie,
S'elle peult, elle se deslie.
Quant donc par plaisir voluntaire
Chantee me fut ceste omelie,
Estoit il lors temps de moy taire?

Se feusse des hoirs Hue Cappel,
Qui fut extrait de boucherie,
On ne m'eust, parmy ce drappel,
Fait boire en ceste escorcherie.
Vous entendez bien joncherie?
Mais quant ceste paine arbitraire
On me jugea par tricherie,
Estoit il lors temps de moy taire?

Cuidiez vous que soubz mon cappel
N'y eust tant de philosophie
Comme de dire: <<J'en appel>>?
Si avoit, je vous certiffie,
Combien que point trop ne m'y fie.
Quant on me dist, present notaire:
<<Pendu serez!>> je vous affie,
Estoit il lors temps de moy taire?

Prince, se j'eusse eu la pepie,
Pieça je feusse ou est Clotaire,
Aux champs debout comme une espie.
Estoit il lors temps de moy taire?

BALLAD TO THE COURT CLERK

How's that for a petition? Good?
Eh Garnier? And did I show
My sense? Like all the rest I would
Stick by my hide. What beast is slow
If it can clear a trap to go?
And when my homily was sung,
Death for a fluke, and whether or no,
Was I then to mind my tongue?

If mine were such a butcher's blood
As noble Capet arteries flow
From Hugh down, then I had not stood
In shambles, gagged to undergo
The water torture. But you know,
Without the wink, what jokes are sprung
On wretches here. Duped, sentenced so,
Was I then to mind my tongue?

You reasoned, did you, that I would
Have bagged too little wit below
My hood to spell appeal? I could
At a pinch muster that much though.
I knew Court said: You shall be hung,
And I knew the notary sealed it so.
Was I then to mind my tongue?

Prince, if pip ailed me, long ago
I should have rotted upright, strung
With scarecrows in the fields a-row.
Was I then to mind my tongue?

CHANSON

Au retour de dure prison,
Ou j'ai laissié presque la vie,
Se Fortune a sur moy envie,
Jugiez s'elle fait mesprison!
Il me semble que, par raison,
Elle deust bien estre assouvie
Au retour.

Se si plaine est de desraison
Que veuille que du tout devie,
Plaise a Dieu que l'ame ravie
En soit lassus en sa maison,
Au retour!

SONG

At length stolen home from that harsh cell
Where all but breath was spent,
Will Fate not now relent?
If no, does she do well? –
When by such ills as fell,
Malice itself is spent,
    At length.

If so her madness swell,
As she's on murder bent,
God catch the soul that's rent,
In his own house to dwell,
    At length.

ÉPITAPHE

CY GIST ET DORT EN CE SOLLIER,
QU'AMOURS OCCIST DE SON RAILLON,
UNG POVRE PETIT ESCOLLIER,
QUI FUT NOMMÉ FRANÇOYS VILLON.
ONCQUES DE TERRE N'EUT SILLON.
IL DONNA TOUT, CHASCUN LE SCET :
TABLES, TRESTEAULX, PAIN, CORBEILLON.
GALLANS, DICTES EN CE VERSET :

> Repos eternel donne a cil,
> Sire, et clarté perpetuelle,
> Qui vaillant plat ni escuelle
> N'eut oncques, n'ung brain de percil.
> Il fut rez, chief, barbe et sourcil,
> Comme ung navet qu'on ret ou pelle.
> Repos eternel donne a cil.
>
> Rigueur le transmit en exil
> Et luy frappa au cul la pelle,
> Nón obstant qu'il dit: «J'en appelle!»
> Qui n'est pas terme trop subtil.
> Repos eternel donne a cil.

EPITAPH AND RONDEL

Here slumbering in sod shall lie
A man for grief of love undone;
The little scholar penny-shy,
Once as François Villon known.
A furrow never was his own,
Yet he must all he had put by,
Till bench, board, tray, and loaf were gone.
Gallants, his last rondel try:

God give him rest in Paradise,
And clarity perpetual.
No dish or platter of least size
He owned on earth; not wherewithal
For parsley sprigs; let his hair fall,
And bald as a peeled turnip lies.
God give him rest in Paradise.

Need shut his Paris from his eyes,
Banished, and kicked him bare of all,
Though mercy, mercy, he would call,
And was not one to mince his cries.
God give him rest in Paradise.

BALLADE DE MERCY

A Chartreux et a Celestins,
A Mendians et a Devotes,
A musars et claquepatins,
A servans et filles mignotes
Portans surcotz et justes cotes,
A cuidereaux d'amours transsis
Chaussans sans meshaing fauves botes,
Je crie a toutes gens mercis.

A filletes monstrans tetins
Pour avoir plus largement d'ostes,
A ribleurs, mouveurs et hutins,
A bateleurs, traynans marmotes,
A folz, folles, a sotz et sotes,
Qui s'en vont siflant six a six,
A marmosetz et mariotes,
Je crie a toutes gens mercis.

Sinon aux traistres chiens matins,
Qui m'ont fait chier dures crostes
Maschier mains soirs et mains matins,
Qu'ores je ne crains pas trois crotes.
Je feisse pour eulx petz et rotes;
Je ne puis, car je suis assis.
Au fort, pour eviter riotes,
Je crie a toutes gens mercis.

Qu'on leur froisse les quinze costes
De gros mailletz, fors et massis,
De plombees et telz pelotes.
Je crie a toutes gens mercis.

BALLAD CRAVING PARDON

Cloister brothers, almoners,
Nuns at worship, mumpers, staid
Patten-clinkers, servitors,
Light-to-come-by girls displayed
In fine jackets snugly made,
Fops who keep a lover's vow
And mincing fawny boots parade,
I would have all your pardons now.

Bare-breasted wenches, barterers
Enticing by your stock-in-trade,
Picklocks, nightly roisterers,
Whistling clowns in bells arrayed,
Simpletons for folly paid,
Men instructing apes to bow,
Little grinning boy and maid,
I would have all your pardons now.

All, all, except those traitor curs',
Who so long upon dry crusts made
Me gnaw, today like scavengers
I am with a rat's fare well stayed.
I have not time left to upbraid,
And sitting can not anyhow
Belch the respects they should be paid.
I would have all your pardons now.

Comfort their ribs with cudgels made
Of stout oak, leaded; and allow
Substantial girth, or have them weighed:
I would have all your pardons now.

BALLADE POUR SERVIR DE CONCLUSION

Icy se clost le testament
Et finist du pauvre Villon.
Venez a son enterrement,
Quant vous orrez le carrillon,
Vestus rouge com vermillon,
Car en amours mourut martir:
Ce jura il sur son couillon,
Quant de ce monde voult partir.

Et je croy bien que pas n'en ment;
Car chassié fut comme ung souillon
De ses amours hayneusement,
Tant que, d'icy a Roussillon,
Brosse n'y a ne brossillon
Qui n'eust, ce dit il sans mentir,
Ung lambeau de son cotillon,
Quant de ce monde voult partir.

Il est ainsi et tellement
Quant mourut n'avoit qu'ung haillon;
Qui plus, en mourant, mallement
L'espoignoit d'Amours l'esguillon;
Plus agu que le ranguillon
D'ung baudrier luy faisoit sentir
(C'est de quoy nous esmerveillon),
Quant de ce monde voult partir.

Prince, gent comme esmerillon,
Sachiez qu'il fist au departir:
Ung traict but de vin morillon,
Quant de ce monde voult partir.

BALLAD BY WAY OF ENDING

Here close his testament and lay,
And Villon, too, is sped.
Bury him upon a day
When the bells ring for the dead;
All that mourn him robed in red.
For he died of love they tell,
Swore to it on his deathbed,
Then to this world farewell.

I think it was no lie to say.
Like an old clout he was shed
By his love and packed away.
From here to Roussillon, he said,
No little bush but by some thread
Or rag it got of him can tell
How far from cruel love he fled.
Then to this world farewell.

So it came, in such a way,
That he died in scarce a shred.
Still love spied him where he lay,
Found him there in dying bed,
And the fiercer arrow sped.
Wonder on his watchers fell:
He nearly felt love's dart when dead.
Then to this world farewell.

Prince that art a falcon bred,
Thus his leave of us befell:
A last drink that was crimson red;
Then to this world farewell.

APPENDIX

BALLADE OF GOOD ADVICE
TO ROGUES

Do you play the pardoner, do you throw
   A dice that's loaded or darkly pore
To make flash money? You'll burn, I trowe,
   As sure as a damn'd conspirator.
   On foggy nights by the tavern door
Do you feel for a purse or a throat to slit?
   What are you filling your wallet for?
Wine and the women take all of it.

Is it lute or flute or the fiddle-bow
   You ply for money, or do you score
From gaping burghers with eyes too slow
   To follow the feint of a conjurer?
   Do you mime a tale out of Bible-lore?
With a five-aced pack do you make your bit?
   It'll all go too as it went before –
Wine and the women take all of it.

What's ill-gotten will bring you woe,
   'Twill find you merry and leave you sore:
Then turn your hand to a steadfast plowe,
   Burn your books on the threshing-floor:
   Thus at ease in your bed you'll snore.
But if from labour you up and quit,
   You're a fool more damn'd than you were before –
Wine and the women take all of it.

ENVOI

The gaudy raiment that once you wore,
   Your robes of satin, your hosen knit,
It'll go again as it went before –
   Wine and the women take all of it.

Translation by Wilfred Thorley

ABCDEFGHIJKLMNOPQRSTUVWXYZ

Two thousand copies of

The Lyrical Poems of François Villon

have been printed on Curtis Rag paper by The Meriden
Gravure Company and bound in cloth imported from the
Netherlands especially for this edition. The type has been
composed by The Stinehour Press in Lunenburg, Vermont;
it is the first book set by that press using Galliard, a new
typeface designed by Matthew Carter. Galliard is based on
the work of the vigorous and original sixteenth-century
punchcutter Robert Granjon, who supplied punches to
Christopher Plantin and other master printers. The Galliard
roman is patterned on Granjon's Gros Cicero and Giubilate
types, while the italic follows his Ascendonica Cursive of
1570. The ornaments from which the endpapers are composed
were adapted, from Renaissance originals, by Matthew Carter for Mergenthaler; Carter's versions appear here for the
first time in a printed book. The typography, calligraphy,
decorative endleaves, and binding were designed by
Stephen Harvard, who here signs

Stephen Harvard

this copy which is number
351